Sir Redvers Buller

Biography of the British Army Commander and Hero of the Second Boer War

By Lewis Butler

PANTIANOS
CLASSICS

Published by Pantianos Classics

ISBN-13: 978-1-78987-172-2

First published in 1909

General The Right Hon. Sir Redvers Buller –
Colonel-Commandment Royal Rifle Corps

Contents

Preface.. *v*

Sir Redvers Buller **6**

One - Introductory.. 6

Two – Early Years.. 7

Three - First Appointment 10

Four - Canada 13

Five – The Red River Expedition................................... 18

Six – The Staff College 23

Seven – South Africa 26

Eight – The 2nd Battalion.. 32

Nine – Egypt, 1882 35

Ten - Ireland 39

Eleven - Aldershot 44

Twelve - Home 69

Thirteen – Retirement in Downes.................................. 73

Fourteen – The Last Moments 76

Fifteen – 'Soldier Rest, Thy Warfare O'er' 81

Preface

The following pages have for the most part already appeared in the 'Chronicle' of the King's Royal Rifle Corps. Hence the regimental tone and allusions throughout.

The little memoir does not, of course, pretend to be a biography — that will be written in due course by a master hand — it is merely the slightest possible sketch of Sir Redvers Buller's career.

I am deeply grateful to Lady Audrey Buller for her permission to reproduce Sir Redvers' letter of 3rd March 1900, and to the many others who have kindly given me their invaluable help.

L. W. B.
April 1909.

Sir Redvers Buller

Colonel Commandant
The King's Royal Rifle Corps

One - Introductory

'Great men are the noblest possession of a nation, and are potent forces in the moulding of national character. Their influence lives after them, and if they be good as well as great they remain as beacons lighting the course of all who follow them.' — Mr. Bryce at Springfield, U.S.A. (Lincoln Centenary), February 12th, 1909.

Redvers Buller! I care not how many titles and distinctions he bore. It was by this name that we knew and loved him. Tons of the 60th he was not the Privy Councillor, not the Knight Grand Cross of the Bath, but simply Redvers Buller, keenest and greatest of Riflemen. It is hard to believe that in this world we have lost him, that we shall no more see that massive figure, that reflective brow, that wonderfully penetrating eye lighting up the kindly countenance, nor hear that voice ever breathing the most profound common sense, whether in homely remarks, in humour, in satire, or in apt repartee,

I cannot pretend to the intimacy with him that many can claim, nor have I known him as long. Still, nearly thirty years have passed since I first met Sir Redvers, when, in the autumn of 1879, immediately after the Zulu War, he came to stay with the 1st Battalion of the 60th at Winchester. He was not an unusually tall man, but something about him gave the impression of great height and heroic proportions. His features were rugged, yet after a few minutes' talk the plainness was forgotten in the marvellous strength of expression and in the intellectual countenance. It was not until the autumn of life that the innate kindliness of his nature assumed predominance in softening the harshness of feature.

In December of the following year I met Colonel Buller at a shooting party in a Cornish country house, and then, for the first time, began to know something of him. It happened that one night we went upstairs together and began chatting in his bedroom. What struck me most, both then and ever afterwards, was his extraordinary power of putting one at one's ease. The enormous difference in our positions was forgotten in an instant, and I felt as though I were talking to my most intimate friend. Hitherto, I had seen that he was a fine shot and noticed that whenever he joined the party in the smoking-room he had a book in his hand, and would often remain absorbed in it regardless of the buzz of conversation around; but now, as he talked, I began to grasp his depth and independence of thought, and his singular power of lucid expression. I felt (and on the few subsequent occasions on which I had any private talk with him I always felt the same) that his conversation was as stimulating to the mind as champagne to the body. It seemed to force the listener to give expression to his own thoughts and ideas; and, however crude those might be, he always paid attention and commented on them with the greatest kindness.

Two – Early Years

Redvers Henry Buller, son of a Devonshire squire, M.P. for a division of the county, owner of the manor of Downes, near Crediton, was born on the 7th December 1839. When only eight years old he was sent to a private school, the head master of which was no doubt a Horatian scholar, and seems to have reflected in his own person the qualities of Orbilius.

"Walking one day down the street, young Buller thought it capital fun to ring the front-door bells as he passed. Being unfortunately detected by the schoolmaster, he was asked in an angry tone, 'Is this to be an institution for gentlemen or not?' 'That depends,' said the boy, perfectly prepared to argue the point, but his defence was interrupted by the production of a stick with which the poor child was unmercifully chastised.

'During the holidays,' observes Mr. Edmund Gosse in a character study, 'he was always in the open air, neglecting his books a good deal, but learning steadily and eagerly in the classes of the Ecole Buissonniere. He spent his early days at Downes among the farm labourers, with the woodman, the blacksmith and the carpenter, and before he went to Eton had managed to pick up a knowledge of many technical things connected with those occupations, so thorough that it has remained with him ever since...His soldiers have often expressed surprise at his practical knowledge. For instance, in the Zulu war a gun-wagon got jambed in being taken through a deep defile. When the manoeuvre seemed hopeless Sir Redvers got down and showed how the thing was to be done. The men could not help expressing amazement. "Oh," replied the General, "it is only a knack! I learned it from watching the woodmen in the Devonshire lanes when I was a boy!"

The Buller family were Harrovians, and Redvers in due course went there, but his stay was brief; for having shocked the excellent pedagogue at that time head master by breaking a window, painting a door red, or some such boyish freak, his parents removed him and sent him forthwith to Eton. Eton has its faults, but its head masters are usually men of the world and do not look with too stern an eye on the exuberance of boyish spirits.

At the house of the Rev. W. B. Marriott, he became the fag of a boy of the greatest distinction, now known as the Rev. Edmond Warre, D.D., lately head master of the College. Dr. Warre — not entirely to one's surprise — remarks that he was a very solid, sturdy person, who had a will of his own not always identical with that of his seniors. Buller seems to have been a fair classical scholar — when a General Officer he could quote Virgil aptly, for he had had no difficulty in learning by heart — and on a memorable occasion in after life showed the value of the watermanship acquired on the Thames. Otherwise there are no remarkable traditions connected with his Eton career, nor do I remember his making any reference to it except to recall a favourite anthem, and the fact that he never smoked after leaving school. He was happy, but with his own pursuits, and did not specially distinguish himself either in games or lessons.

When just sixteen terrible sorrow overtook him. On his way home for the Christmas holidays, his mother met him at Exeter station. The boy noticed blood on the platform and on her pocket handkerchief. Hemorrhage of the lungs had set in. She was taken into the waiting-room, where a bed was hastily improvised. Young Redvers stood over his mother, giving her relief by fanning her steadily for hours together. Bystanders wondered at his powers of endurance. The boy remained with his mother all night. She could never be moved, and died in the waiting-room a day or two afterwards.

'It was at Eton,' says Mr. Gosse, in the same sketch, 'and towards the end of his school life, that he determined, quite independently, to go into the Army; but just before joining his regiment he very nearly put an end to everything. He was up in a tree in the woods at Downes, lopping, when he cut his right leg so severely that the Devonshire doctor declared it must be amputated or else he would die. Redvers Buller stoutly replied that he would rather die with two legs than live with one, and he was eventually cured. It, however, slightly hampered his movements and made him a little less agile than he would otherwise have been.' He had a passion for hunting, rough as it was in those days, acquired a good seat, and rode well to the Tremlett Hounds.

Three - First Appointment

On the 23rd May 1858 Buller was gazetted as Ensign in the 2nd Battalion of the 60th Rifles. On the 14th July, three lads, C. Gosling, A. Borthwick, and Arthur Morris, joined the Rifle Depot at Winchester. Late in the evening a fourth made his appearance, and, as if to assert his independence at the very outset, dined at mess in his travelling clothes. It was Redvers Buller. In the early days of his service he does not seem to have gone out of the way to ingratiate himself either with his seniors or contemporaries. He was respected, for he showed great force of character, but was, perhaps, hardly among the most generally popular. He was very contradictory, and rather irritated people by his love of argument, though it was admitted that there was always force in his assertions; and being addicted to laying down the law he gained the sobriquet of 'The Judge.' [1] He was fond of horses, fond also of cards.

Early in January 1859, Buller sailed to join his Battalion in India. Disembarking at Alexandria he went overland to Suez, where he again took ship for Calcutta, and saw no more of Egypt until the war of 1882. He joined the head-quarter wing of his Battalion at Benares, going up thither by bullock train, in command of a convoy of women and children. At one of the halting places, where there was no doctor, a woman asked the young ensign to prescribe for her baby who was suffering from a slight ailment. Buller was a little at a loss, but, after mature reflection, informed the mother that in his own case, on similar occasions, he found the restringent power of port wine. The woman eagerly took his advice and the baby was given a glass of port, with results which, it is to be hoped, were to its advantage!

The last embers of the Mutiny were not, at that time, entirely stamped out, and flying columns still scoured the country. But though the conditions must have been very much those of active service, it does not appear that young Buller saw any shot fired.

One who was at that time a subaltern in the 60th writes: 'What struck me most with Buller was his determination and the perfect control he had over his temper, so great indeed that I wondered if he had a temper or not, and often tried to get it out, but having on one occasion succeeded, I did not try again. I remember an instance in which he showed this determination and self-control in conquering a vicious horse. At Benares there was at that time a very fine horse known as the Man-eater, having killed two syces, and as his name implies, a perfect devil. His trick was to rear at the moment he was mounted and throw himself back on his rider; then — cat-like — get on his feet so quickly as to be able to tackle the rider on the ground with his fore feet and teeth. Buller bought him for ten rupees and started to teach him manners. I was present, I think, on every occasion until the cure was complete. The *modus operandi* was as follows: The horse was brought out of his stables by three syces, one with a twitch on his lip and the others with a twitch on his ear. He was saddled with an ordinary hunting saddle, and had a strong snaffle bridle and a slip rein from the knee D at each side of the saddle through the ring of the bit, thence through a ring on the martingale, and up and over the neck. Buller in breeches, gaiters, and spurs, but with no whip, got into the saddle with some difficulty, took the slip rein in his left and the ordinary rein in his right, nodding to the syces to let go, and immediately pressing the horse with his knees to go on. In a second the animal tried to rear, bat his head was pulled down between his knees by the slip rein and the spurs driven into him, when he plunged and kicked for a good five minutes. The moment he quieted a little, the pressure of the knee was again applied, and the scene repeated itself over and over again for more than an hour, when at last, on receiving the pressure of the knee, he gave in and went quietly where required. Every morning for a week this performance went on, except that each morning the horse gave in sooner, and I think it was on the sixth morning that he gave in without a battle, and never again attempted to rear with Buller on his back. I have never witnessed such an exhibition of coolness and determination on the part of a rider.'

On the 28th February 1860, the Battalion embarked for China, Ensign Buller being on board the *Hougoumont*. He never visited India again. Twenty years later, when on the point of embarking to join the same Battalion in Afghanistan, he was stopped by order of the Duke of Cambridge. In 1893 he was pressed to accept, but declined, the post of Commander-in-Chief in India.

After a few weeks spent in Stanley Barracks at Hong Kong, the Battalion re-embarked to join the combined British and French force assembling at Talien Bay, in the Gulf of Pechili, with a view to the enforcement of the treaty made with the Chinese Government two years previously. [2] Preparations being complete, the Army once more embarked on the 24th July, and on the 1st August landed unopposed at Pehtang, twelve miles north of Taku. In the subsequent brief campaign, which ended in the occupation of Pekin, the only two things recorded of Buller are that the rank and file of his company were devoted to him, and that he quarrelled the whole time with his Captain. As the latter was not the wisest of men the fact does not entirely take one by surprise. Buller could have seen but little fighting, and for years afterwards refused to wear the Chinese medal. Still he did gain his 'baptism of fire,' and a letter from him gives a quiet and dispassionate account of his first action, showing that he was as cool at nineteen as in after life.

During his stay in China two misadventures attended the ensign. He was so nearly drowned that he was thought dead when pulled out of the water: and a horse kicked out his front teeth, thus making his speech a little indistinct for the rest of his life.

The 60th was the last regiment to leave Pekin on the 9th November, when it marched to Tien-tsin. At this place it was cut off by the ice and forced to remain through the winter. It was not until the end of September 1861 that the Battalion — having lost by death 101 N.C.O.'s and men — went down the Pei-ho river in gunboats and embarked for England in the *Simoom*, which eventually sailed from Hong Kong on the 2nd November. The ship encountered a hurricane soon after starting, and looked like going down. A passenger remarks: 'There was not a movement on deck, eleven hundred men awaiting the result calmly and steadily, although they knew every moment might be their last.' On the 3rd January 1862 it touched at the Cape of Good Hope, and Buller got his first glimpse of the country upon which he was destined to leave so indelible a mark. We have seen that on his voyage out he had landed in Egypt. It is curious that in his first tour of foreign service he should have visited the two countries which eventually proved to be the principal scenes of his future distinction. Spithead was not reached until the 24th February, after a voyage little short of four months.

[1] What actually gave rise to the name was his quotation of his ancestor Judge Buller' s dictum, 'The greater the truth the greater the libel.' To his brother subalterns Redvers seemed entitled to be called Judge Buller no less than was his forebear.

[2] The British force was commanded by Lieut. -General Sir Hope Grant. In a number of the *Illustrated London News* of that date may be found a picture of the General and his staff. Among the latter is a short individual of hirsute appearance, and adorned, to his evident satisfaction, with a pair of the enormous whiskers known as 'Piccadilly weepers.' The name underneath is Colonel Wolseley! Those who have only known the trim Field-Marshal in later life would be puzzled to find any resemblance to their friend, who, by the way, states in his autobiography that this was the best managed campaign he ever saw.

Four - Canada

The Battalion remained at Portsmouth in the Cambridge Barracks, but Buller's period of home service was short. Being promoted in December to the rank of Lieutenant, he joined at Quebec the 4th Battalion, commanded by that foremost of Riflemen, Colonel R. B. Hawley. The enormous advantage to a young man of serving under a first-rate commanding officer can perhaps be best realised by those who have not been equally fortunate. Were it not that Colonel Hawley's life and character will shortly be the theme of an abler pen, one might be tempted into a digression. Suffice it to remark that his light infantry practice was taken from that of the 5th Battalion of the 60th, which served throughout the Peninsular War, and on being disbanded bequeathed it to the 1st Battalion. It was as true of Hawley as of his prototype, Sir John Moore, the centenary of whose death falls this year, that 'the officers were formed for command and soldiers acquired such discipline as to become an example to the army and proud of their profession. Though drill was an important part of the instruction it was not by that alone that the soldier was formed. It was the internal and moral system, the constant superintendence of the officers, the real government and responsibility of the captains which carried the discipline to such perfection.' Every single thing connected with the food, comfort, and training of a regiment was brought by Hawley to its highest pitch of perfection. His system, like that of Sir John Moore, was based on the cultivation of the morale and self-reliance of the individual. Among his many distinguished pupils may be mentioned Lord Grenfell, Sir Edward Hutton, General Terry, Colonel Donald Browne, Colonel Montagu Walker, and Captain Brownrigg, but the most brilliant of all was Redvers Buller himself. Lord Wolseley was not more *facile princeps* on the Staff side of the Army than was Hawley on the Regimental.

Buller had a carpenter's bench fitted in his barrack-room, and always found time to do something useful instead of loafing. Whatever he did was done thoroughly and on sound principle. He was devoted to fishing, and, being clever with his fingers, was an adept at tying salmon flies. His accomplishments in general were very varied. It was, e.g., noticed that he could point out at a glance the colours appropriate to any particular room, or even describe the details of a lady's dress. It was indeed observed of him that he was particularly sensitive to colour, and the observer remarked that 'this faculty is but one manipulation of a mind the genius of which lies in great part in its orderly arrangement, its absolute sureness of movement. In later life he was fond of urging on young men the cultivation of the eye, which he thought could be deliberately studied and mastered, even when there is no natural gift for it.' His instincts and interests at this period were sporting rather than military. He spent his winters on hunting expeditions in the company of a few Indians, and became an expert in the art of the backwoodsman. All his plans were well thought out. For this education in what he called the 'hunter's instinct,' which proved an excellent foundation for a more purely military training, Canada was an unequalled school. Colonel Hawley was not a man to allow any officer to neglect his work, and in any case Buller's sense of duty was far too great to let him do so. He probably, without knowing it, became by degrees a soldier. At all events in 1867 we find him in a post of responsibility. As 'look out' officer in "Western Canada, his duty was to visit selected soldiers posted at the frontier stations in order to prevent deserters crossing the border into the United States. This involved a great deal of travelling, during which he gained experience in various ways.

An old friend writes: 'I first met him when travelling by train from St. John's, New Brunswick, to London, Canada West. He came up to me and said, "Is your name H ___? I see by your baggage you are joining my regiment, so come into my carriage and I will put you up to the ways of the country." This was an instance of his great good-nature and of looking after the helpless. In society Buller was a great favourite. Girls idolised him though so blunt in speech, but always with a laugh. Among the regimental institutions of that date was a pack of hounds. Donald Browne was master, Redvers Buller a whipper in. When we got under trees where the crust of twenty feet deep snow was so soft that the big foxhounds sank up to their middles and could not flounder along, Buller would take a hound under each arm and snow-shoe to a harder surface. In the hot summer four of us drove out to fish, and getting into impenetrably thick bush had to walk. The two men carrying the big basket of provisions were soon "done" by the heat, mosquitoes, and sandflies, so Buller took it from them, put it on his own shoulders, and walked off with it. What struck me was his extraordinary energy, fearlessness of any authority, wiriness and good temper, and nothing seemed to escape him.'

In the messroom Buller would love an argument, always taking the unpopular side. He liked to contradict people in order to elicit their reasons for an assertion, and had no objection to be contradicted himself. In his conversation he was a very Palace of Truth; but his apt, though sometimes uncomplimentary remarks were always accompanied by a laugh which deprived them of half their sting. If, in his opinion, however, occasion demanded it, he could show that he was not to be trifled with. An officer who had come to us from another regiment and had disgraced himself, ventured to look at a game of billiards through the glass door of the ante-room. Buller gave him a hint that he was not wanted, and the hint being ignored, followed it up by catching hold of the back of a chair and driving the four legs through the glass.

It was at this period that he first made the acquaintance of Lord Wolseley, at that time Assistant Adjutant-General in Canada. Of their first meeting I have heard three irreconcilable accounts. That to which I give credit states that Buller, desirous of an interview with the General in Command, was stopped by Colonel Wolseley, who told him that the General was unable to see him. The subaltern, however, insisted that he *would* see him, and so he did.

The years which followed were possibly the most important of Buller's life. He went out to Canada a raw and self-willed young man, with perhaps no great interest in his profession. He returned to England a trained and experienced soldier. The moulding of his character must be put down to Hawley's gentle guidance. A shrewd judge of men, the latter quickly discerned real genius underlying the new-comer's somewhat rough exterior, while Buller at the same time discovered to what heights the art of training and administering a regiment could be raised. Colonel and subaltern became fast friends. In spite of the difference in age they associated with each other. One day they were in a canoe together near rapids. Hawley pointed them out and wished to disembark, but Buller, in his self-confident way, refused to admit the danger. The force of the current increased; the peril became undeniable. 'We had better go to the shore and get out,' said Buller. 'No,' returned the Colonel; 'I have come so far for your pleasure, you will now kindly go on for mine.' A quarrel in the canoe would have meant instant death, and Buller was forced to obey. The rapids were shot and safely passed. But the incident was never forgotten by tutor or pupil.

Lieutenant R. H. Buller and Colonel Hawley (60th Rifles) At Montreal

Colonel Hawley had broken in the colt, and in doing so had conceived the greatest admiration for him.

One day in the year 1868 the Adjutant, Lieut. Brownrigg, was going home on leave. The Colonel asked Buller to undertake the duties in his absence. Buller protested, saying that the one thing he knew nothing about was soldiering. 'I will teach you,' replied Hawley; and after thinking over the offer for twenty-four hours, Buller accepted it. This was the turning-point of his life.

Having made the plunge, he became as fond of soldiering as of sport. The Colonel and his Acting-Adjutant were more inseparable than ever. Hawley, with great tact, often asked Buller for his opinion, and Buller was never reluctant to give it; sometimes perhaps with undue freedom, for he always spoke his mind to anyone and everyone in the most uncompromising way, and a sense of subordination to his superiors was not one of his strong points. On one occasion a difference of opinion as to the promotion of a sergeant took place, and Buller remarked, 'Of course, as Colonel you can do as you like, but you will destroy the company! 'For the next fortnight they only addressed each other officially, but it was merely a lovers' quarrel. Hawley came into the ante-room one afternoon and said, 'Buller, I want you to come out for a walk with me.' They returned the best of friends, for Buller thoroughly realised that Hawley was a master of his art and a generation in advance of his age. At a regimental dinner many years later he observed that although Hawley had come to us from another regiment, he had, in an infinitesimally short time, been voted the finest Rifleman in the world; and added that the manoeuvres embodied in the Field Exercises for the first time in 1896 had been habitually practised by the 4th Battalion of the 60th in 1862.

Five – The Red River Expedition

By the time Brownrigg returned Buller was thoroughly imbued with love of his profession. He felt disappointment that he had no opportunity of becoming the actual Adjutant. But his turn for promotion was now at hand. The 4th Battalion came home in the summer of 1869, but in May of the following year Buller, after twelve years' service, was gazetted Captain and posted to the 1st Battalion, at that time assembling in Thunder Bay, Lake Superior, for the Red River Expedition. He was not very anxious to join it. He was convinced that there would be no fighting, and having been abroad during nearly eleven of the previous twelve years, felt perhaps that he was entitled to a little home service. But his hesitation was brief, and the 10th June found him at Thunder Bay.

The circumstances of the problem about to be solved were rather curious. The Hudson Bay Company, by virtue of its original Charter, claimed possession of the whole Dominion of Canada to the north and west of the province of Ontario. The claim was, of course, inadmissible, and such rights as those to which it was in reality entitled had been bought in 1869 by the Government of Canada. But some of the French Canadians still contended that the country was not legally under British rule. One Riel raised the standard of revolt at Fort Garry, a trading station of the Hudson Bay Company, near the town of Winnipeg. Englishmen boast of their capacity for business; Frenchmen exercise it. What Kiel was now doing was merely the traditional French policy of establishing a line of forts behind British settlements, thus confining them to the sea coast and excluding them from the hinterland.

Colonel — now Field-Marshal Lord — Wolseley was appointed to command the British force, which consisted of the 1st Battalion of the 60th Rifles and two battalions of Canadian Militia. The distance from Thunder Bay to Fort Garry by the river route was over 600 miles. After the first few miles of road the whole journey was to be done by boat. The route ran, not along sluggish streams and calm lakes, but through foaming rapids studded with sunken rocks, in which the most wary steersman could hardly find a passage. Canadian voyageurs were provided, but Buller quickly found that he knew a great deal more of boat craft than they did; and although the Government maps were faulty to the last degree, and his own for a considerable distance was the foremost boat, he took the helm himself and successfully steered through the intricate and almost impenetrable channels. Anon the course lay along the surface of a lake: smoother indeed than the river, but sometimes lashed into fury by wind and storm, and so densely dotted with islands and indented by creek and bay that it was almost impossible to see whether the true channel was being threaded or whether the helmsman was unwittingly steering for the shore. Here Captain Buller's boating experience in Eton days stood him in good stead. Noticing one night that the water ahead — which shone clear in the moonlight — was dead calm for some miles, while rippled water could be seen through an opening between islands, he instantly judged that the latter must be the true course, and turning sharp to the right gained the proper channel, while every other boat's crew, accompanied by a less competent guide, going straight on, found itself headed off by the shore and had a five-mile row round the bay.

Every now and again the head of the lake or river would be reached and a portage would have to be crossed. Boats were emptied of their stores and hauled over rollers to the next point of embarkation, perhaps a mile or two distant, while the rifles, food, &c, were carried on the backs of the crew. In such work Buller was unsurpassed. Lord Wolseley remarks that, 'All the officers of the expeditionary force soon became expert in making portages and in mending their boats, no one more so than my able friend and valued comrade, Redvers Buller. It was here that I first made his acquaintance, and I am proud to feel that we have been firm friends ever since. He was a first-rate axe-man, and I think he was the only man with us of any rank who could carry a 100-lb. barrel of pork on his back. [1] He could mend a boat and have her back in the water with her crew and all her stores on board whilst many would have been still making up their minds what to do. Full of resource, and personally absolutely fearless, those serving under him always trusted him fully.' Six boats conveyed Buller's company. That of his subaltern, Lieut. Burstall, had its stern literally torn out by a rock; but with the aid of canvas, white lead, and a covering of tin Buller himself mended it, as indeed he mended all the other boats of his company, which were constantly knocking up against rocks. His own boat was, however, absolutely unhurt from start to finish.

Through Rainy Lake and Lake of the Woods (bordered sometimes by romantic scenery, sometimes by arid desolation) rowed the convoy after crossing the watershed dividing the streams which flow into Lake Superior from those which flow into Hudson Bay; and then reached along the terrible Winnipeg river. Here even Buller's science might have been at fault, but he had happily just been joined by a first-rate Indian guide, and after eleven days of incredibly hard work, Fort Alexander, a Hudson Bay post on the east bank of Lake Winnipeg, was reached, and the perils of the voyage were over. Splendidly as the Riflemen had worked — mostly in torrents of rain — Buller thought the men of the 1st Battalion less handy than those of the 4th — they had not had Hawley's training — but he said they had a grand tradition of Delhi and earlier campaigns which carried them through everything. Riel's stronghold, Fort Garry, was reached on the 24th. It was already deserted. The birds had flown. But so much had they been taken by surprise, and so narrow was the margin for escape, that Kiel's unfinished breakfast still lay on the table. The band played the regimental march as the Riflemen entered the fort — the two regiments of Canadian Militia had not yet come up — and to the accompaniment of the National Anthem, the Union Jack was hoisted on the walls. From the further bank of the river two men stood watching the ceremony. It afterwards turned out that they were Riel and his secretary! Not a shot was fired from start to finish, and Buller caustically remarked that he was disgusted at having come so far to hear the band play 'God Save the Queen.' But, although Buller was unconscious of the fact or indeed of having done anything out of the common, the Red River Expedition was everything to him. He had trained himself in the backwoods and Colonel Hawley had trained him in the details of his profession. This was his first opportunity of reaping the fruits of both, and in doing so he was fortunate in coming under the eye of the rising soldier of the day. Magnificently as the whole Battalion, commanded by Colonel Randal Feilden and led by good captains, had done, Colonel Wolseley quickly singled out Redvers Buller; and he recommended him and Captain John Owen Young — another excellent officer — for promotion to the brevet rank of major. But the Horse Guards authorities decided that, as there had been no fighting, the brevets must be given to the two senior captains, irrespective of merit. The temporary loss of brevet rank made no difference to Buller: he was placed on Wolseley' s list of able men and thenceforward proved himself indispensable. But even this did not represent the true measure of his success. His feats of strength, his surpassing skill, his *coup d'oeil*, caused the Riflemen to look upon him as something superhuman; while his thought for everyone but himself, and his wonderful magnetism of sympathy endeared him to their hearts. Those who have heard the old soldiers of the 1st Battalion say with an emphasis impossible to reproduce, 'He was a *gentleman*,' the term of the very highest praise which it is possible for them to use, will bear me out in what might otherwise be thought an exaggeration. And what was the reason of this spell? It was because his men realised that his interests were identical with their own, that there was no barrier of so-called class distinction between them, that he was totally devoid of partiality except for merit, and that, like a true king among men, [2] he could do everything better than they could; that he was in short their truest friend and a model for Riflemen of every age and generation. No wonder that, when asked a few years later his opinion on flogging, he could say, 'I never found any difficulty in maintaining discipline without punishment.' The present is an age in which education is much talked about, if little understood. The opportunities of mutual education afforded by the relations in which officers and men of the 60th and other regiments stand towards each other — more particularly on such occasions as the Red River Expedition — are little appreciated by the world at large

Incredible as it seems, although Fort Garry — to use Lord Wolseley's expression — was as far from a telegraph station as Kent from

Rome, Buller in a letter dated thence on 24th August mentions 'rumours of great European Wars, and the French being licked.' Now, the first defeat of a French Division at Weissemburg had taken place only twenty days previously, while the first general actions at Woerth and Spicheren did not take place until the 6th of the month. Truly a bird of the air had carried the matter! The stay at Fort Garry was very brief. Leaving the Militia regiments in garrison, the 60th began to retrace its steps before the end of August. Captain Buller, with his company, selected for the purpose by Wolseley, greatly shortened the distance by marching overland as far as the northwest angle of the Lake of the Woods, when he again took to his boats, which had been brought round by another company. Nothing further of interest occurred until the Battalion reached Montreal early in October.

[1] Lord Wolseley understates the case. Speaking in a private letter of the very first (the Kashiborine) portage, Captain Buller writes: 'The portage was about three-quarters of a mile long. Over it we had to carry on our backs all our loads, consisting of about twenty-eight barrels a boat, and then to drag the boats over. This took us just a day, and we camped the other end, having finished it. I carried five loads over. I thought them heavy then; they averaged about 100lb. apiece. To show how practice improves one at this work, I should say that, coming down from Winnipeg, my loads over twenty-seven portages seldom averaged less than 180lb., and I carried through without putting down or resting, which at first I had to do every 150 yards or so.' Lieut. St. Maur — the present Duke of Somerset — whose sobriquet, 'Anak,' denoted his herculean size and strength, habitually carried an arm-chest across the portages.
[2] The original meaning" of the word 'king' is one who can do things better than other people.

Six – The Staff College

Thence Buller went home, and though he seems to have returned to Canada in 1871, he was there only a short time. In the meanwhile he had passed into the Staff College, and at the end of the year left his battalion to go through the course. He never again did regimental duty with the 60th.

His life at the Staff College was uneventful. He was a "Whip to the Drag-hounds of which the well-known General Leir-Carleton was the Master. He took a prominent part in the life of the College, and is described as 'a wonderfully clever, clear-headed man, who could play the game all round — in work, hunting, and society — and endowed with a rare fund of anecdote.' Among his contemporaries there the most distinguished in after-life were Sir John Ardagh and Sir William Gatacre. He did not think his prospects very brilliant. He had had fifteen years of service without a chance of distinction, and lamented his fate. But the opportunity was now at hand. In the August of his second year he was studying on the ground the battlefields of the Franco-German War, when he had so vivid a dream of receiving an urgent letter from Sir Garnet Wolseley that he forthwith returned home. Here surely enough he found the letter offering him an appointment on the Staff of the Expeditionary Force to Ashanti. Buller was, however, unwilling to lose the fruit of his work at the Staff College, and it was not until the Commander-in-Chief had decided that for purposes of his profession he should be considered to have graduated that he definitely accepted the appointment in Ashanti. The little campaign that followed was chiefly remarkable for the astonishing number of able men collected by Sir Garnet Wolseley. Colley, Evelyn Wood, Brackenbury, Baker Russell, Alison, Butler, Greaves, Home, Maurice, and many others formed what became known as the 'Ashanti Ring,' a term intended to be one of reproach, but proving in the long run one of the highest praise. 'First and foremost among them as one whose stern determination of character nothing could ruffle, whose resource in difficulty was not surpassed by anyone I ever knew,' says Lord Wolseley in his 'Story of a Soldier's Life,' 'was Redvers Buller Endowed with a mind fruitful in expedients, he inspired general confidence, and thoroughly deserved it. Had a thunderbolt burst at his feet he would have merely brushed from his rifle jacket the earth it had thrown upon him, without any break in the sentence he happened to be uttering at the moment.' [1] It was remarked by regimental officers that Buller had none of the airs which service on the Staff seemed to give to some of his confreres. Sir Garnet Wolseley made him head of the Intelligence Department; and, with the spirit of thoroughness in which he carried out everything he undertook, he at once made a study of the idiosyncrasies of the various native tribes, a study which, at the end of the campaign, was noted by the General in his dispatch as having given him invaluable help in dealing with all the kings and chiefs. While moving a vote of thanks in the House of Commons, Mr. Disraeli, the Premier, said that in spite of the extraordinary difficulties from beginning to end, it was remarkable that the intelligence was wonderfully complete. Continually with the advance guard in the dense forest, often scouting in front of it, Buller carried his life in his hand. Well to the fore during the first fight at Essaman he was struck by a slug, the force of which was happily broken by a hard substance in his pocket. At the fight of Ordashu he was slightly wounded. After the capture of Coomassie he was appointed Prize Agent, and spent the night in the palace, superintending the collection of the silks, gold, ornaments, &c, which formed the booty. His services were frequently acknowledged in Sir Garnet's dispatches, and at the end of the war he received a brevet majority and C. B.

On returning to England Major Buller was appointed Deputy Assistant Adjutant-General at Headquarters. Here he attempted, though with no great success, to inspire the Horse Guards' authorities with Hawley's views on drill and manoeuvre. It was during this period that he took a leading part in the reorganisation of the Naval and Military Club, and established it on the excellent social and financial basis on which it has ever since rested.

[1] Except for the thunderbolt this remark was afterwards verified to the letter in Egypt. A bullet tore away the lace of his sleeve without interrupting the conversation in which he was engaged.

Seven – South Africa

Early in 1878 Buller was asked to go to South Africa on special service with General Thesiger, better known, on the death of his father shortly afterwards, as Lord Chelmsford. The moment was rather a critical one, for Turkey had just been vanquished by Russia after a gallant struggle; the Russians were at the gates of Constantinople, and there seemed every prospect of England becoming involved in the war. Reviewing the circumstances with his usual *sang froid*, Buller, in spite of his friends' remonstrances, decided that England would not be compelled to take an active part, and that, in order to get promotion, he would do well to go to South Africa. His forecast was borne out by the result, and indeed his private correspondence shows many instances of predictions fulfilled almost to the letter.

Among his fellow-passengers on board the *Ambiez* was Lieut. -Colonel — now Field-Marshal Sir Evelyn — Wood. In Cape Colony a Kaffir war was in full swing, and had been already prosecuted with vigour by Thesiger's predecessor, Sir Arthur Cunynghame. Buller was at first sent as Staff Officer to Commandant Frost, a very able Colonial, to whose tuition both at the time and in a public speech in 1899 he acknowledged his obligations; but on the 22nd April was appointed to the command of the Frontier Light Horse, a regiment some 250 strong; a most miscellaneous crew, many of the troopers being surf boatmen from the coast, many foreigners; but with a fine leaven of Dutch Boers, from whom Buller learned a very great deal that was useful. Such a collection could not fail to contain a curious admixture of reputable and disreputable persons. Under anyone else the Frontier Light Horse might have become, as Abercromby said of the Militia in Ireland, a terror to everyone except the enemy. But there was a stern side to Buller's character, and shortly after assuming his command he had occasion to show it. Having had some hard work, the Commanding Officer gave the men a short rest, but knowing they would spend the interval for the most part in a state of intoxication, he warned them to come to parade sober and fit for service in two days' time. The regiment answered to his call pretty well; one man, however, was not only drunk, but actually dared to loudly abuse the C.O. to his face. Buller said nothing except to give the word of command to march; but, having gone a few miles, halted, and then, in the most conspicuous manner possible, ordered the man to dismount, and sent him about his business. The one example sufficed. Insubordination was quelled for ever, and that it took an astonishingly short time to get his regiment in order was due to that splendid element of magnetic sympathy known as 'power of command.' The men felt it personally degrading to do anything the Colonel disliked. At a later period a man misbehaved. He was forgiven. He repeated the offence. He was urged to ask forgiveness again, but he was quite unable to bring himself to do so. 'I cannot,' he moaned piteously, 'I cannot face Buller.'

Mr. Gosse tells us that at a dinner party where Mr. Gladstone was present, some one quoted Joshua as an instance of a soldier the like of whom could not be matched in modern history. Mr. Gladstone in his vehement way took this up at once. 'Joshua, Joshua!' he exclaimed; 'why, Joshua could not hold a candle to Sir Redvers Buller as a leader of men.'

Buller and the Frontier Light Horse became a proverb for everything that was skilful and daring. His own achievements were those of a paladin of old, though it is impossible to get any idea of them from his private letters. At the Perie Bush he surpassed himself. Of his two captains, one was killed and the other desperately wounded. The Kaffirs were at bay among some rocks halfway down the precipitous side of a mountain. They could have been picked off from below, but a company of infantry detailed for the purpose failed to make its appearance. Advancing from the crest, Buller's troopers were repulsed. 'It was,' he says, 'some time before we came again. However, with the help of the Fingoes, we got in and killed all the people inside the rocks, about fifteen; not many, but quite enough to make it hot for us, as there was only room for us to go in two and two at a time.' From this brief notice one would hardly suppose that what actually happened was, that on Evelyn Wood bringing up a company of infantry, Buller, shouting, 'Frontier Light Horse, will you allow the red coats to get in front of you?' made himself into a kind of toboggan, slid down for 40 ft. the precipice which formed the only means of approach amid the concentrated fire of the Kaffirs, and led the attack on the rocks single-handed.

After the action at Taba-ka-Udoda, Buller again distinguished himself by returning to rescue wounded men who had been left behind in a very nasty cave in the Bush. The Kaffirs were subdued by the autumn. For these repeated acts of gallantry Buller was mentioned in Lord Chelmsford's dispatch, and in November received the brevet of Lieutenant-Colonel. He mentions a sixty miles' march in eleven hours, which brought him into Natal; and one of 488 miles in twenty-one days from Maritzburg to Burger's Fort in the Transvaal, via Newcastle and Lydenburg. Here at Lydenburg he awaited the more serious Zulu "War, which was evidently close at hand. [1] The Transvaal Republic, bankrupt in finance and threatened with destruction by its black neighbours, had, in 1877, been incorporated in the British Empire. Among those neighbouring tribes none were better organised or more formidably menacing than the subjects of Cetewayo, King of Zululand, on the eastern border of Natal. To the Zulus, by law and custom of life, war was a necessity. If the British debarred him from fighting the Boers, Cetewayo felt that he had no option but to fight the British. His men were not only hardy in the extreme, but were organised in impis or legions, and highly trained in the art of war. The Zulus could march, manoeuvre, and fight. In January 1879 Lord Chelmsford crossed the frontier of Natal to enforce obedience. A few days later one of his columns was surprised and cut to pieces at Isandhlwana. For a time matters were critical, but Evelyn Wood (who commanded a column with Buller as his lieutenant) held his own; and when reinforcements arrived from England, the tide turned. A reconnaissance of the Inhlobana mountain revealed the enemy in over-whelming force. Buller's orders were not complied with, and he found himself hard pressed on the edge of the mountain with a precipice behind him. The destruction of his whole force seemed inevitable, but with the utmost coolness Buller dismounted his men, pushed the horses by main force down the edge of the steep, and following with his troopers made good his retreat, though with the loss of 100 men. Again and again did Buller go back during the retreat to pick up wounded men, and he received the Victoria Cross, which he had probably earned a dozen times over. The words of the *Gazette* were as follow: —

'For his gallant conduct at the retreat at Inhlobana on the 28th March 1879, in having assisted, while hotly pursued by the Zulus, in rescuing Captain C. D'Arcy of the Frontier Light Horse, who was retiring on foot, and carrying him on his horse until he overtook the rearguard; also for having, on the same date and under the same circumstances, conveyed Lieut. C. Everitt of the F.L.H., whose horse had been killed under him, to a place of safety. Later on Colonel Buller in the same manner saved a trooper of the F.L.H. whose horse was completely exhausted, and who would otherwise have been killed by the Zulus.'

Pursuing its advantage, the Zulu army attacked Wood the follow-ing day at Kambula, but after a hot fight was repulsed, and the re-pulse was turned into a rout by the pursuit of Buller and his caval-ry. To say that during this campaign the Colonel had the entire con-fidence of his men is to understate the case. He was known as the 'Bayard of South Africa,' and was looked on as a hero of heroes for the reason that, as during the Red River and Ashanti expeditions, he thought of everyone but himself. His powers of endurance were remarkable. He was on one occasion in the saddle from 11.30 p.m. till 9 p.m. the next day, and then from 8 a.m. till 5 p.m. on the day following. He habitually reconnoitred ten or fifteen miles in ad-vance of the British cavalry, and, whether in reconnaissance or pursuit, showed every characteristic of that *rara avis*, a cavalry leader. As is the case with every able man, his powers of observation were great. One day he noticed a Zulu shepherd with his flock on the opposite side of a mealie field, and at once halted his party. 'That man,' he remarked, 'would not be there if his friends were not between ns and him.' And so it proved. He is described at this period as 'a silent, saturnine man.' Yet to his friends he was cheery and ready to talk. But he was not a man to stand impertinence. 'I am amused with your advice that I should flatter newspaper correspondents, as only yesterday I had occasion to pull one through a thorn bush to teach him manners,' he writes cheerfully; adding, 'if he revenges himself by caricaturing me, buy a copy of his paper and keep it for me!' Another correspondent, who had been treated with confidence, actually told Colonel Buller that he considered himself justified in reading and making use of any private correspondence he might happen to find, and was surprised next day to be turned out of the Colonel's tent. This man used afterwards to say, 'I hate him and he hates me' (this was a mistake), 'nevertheless he is the greatest genius I have ever met.' On meeting the officer who had accompanied the Prince Imperial on his last ride, Buller's indignation broke out, but his sense of justice led him afterwards to emphasise the fact that the officer had never before been under fire, and to add that he might have done well on the next occasion. The same sense of justice was keenly shown on a court-martial which tried another officer for an error of judgment. Little as he sympathised with his conduct, he drew attention to every point which could tell in the prisoner's favour, and the latter considered that to him he owed his acquittal. His gentleness of character asserted itself also on other occasions. The brother of Cetewayo offered to capitulate with his tribe, on the condition that the women and children received British protection. Wood and Buller rode out to escort them into the British camp. Buller, like a true, fastidious Etonian, loudly declared that nothing would induce him to touch the vermin-covered children. But they had not got far on their return journey before General Wood, looking round, saw Buller with three

30

Zulu babies in front of him on the saddle, and three others perched up behind!

On the day before the battle of Ulundi, Colonel Buller reconnoitred the Zulu position, and determined the ground on which the battle was fought. He fully carried out his intention of discovering the true strength of the enemy, and withdrew his forces with great skill and coolness from a veritable nest of hornets. On the following day the enemy's attack was repelled, and as the Zulus flinched from our fire Lord Chelmsford ordered the British cavalry to charge. After giving the message to the officer concerned, the A.D.C. told Buller of the General's order. Buller, assegai in hand, dashed like lightning with the Frontier Light Horse to the front, driving the Zulus before him in irremediable confusion. A few days later Sir Garnet Wolseley succeeded Lord Chelmsford in command, but Buller came home, for the war was to all intents and purposes at an end, and he was suffering from the effects of a wound which refused to heal. On reaching England the Colonel was summoned to Windsor Castle, where Her Majesty the Queen — the shrewdest judge of character — appreciating his fearless honesty, his modesty, and his somewhat unconventional mode of speech, made him one of her Aides-de-camp [2] and treated him with a kindness and generous confidence which she never abandoned during her life. When he afterwards related the subject of his conversation with the Queen, some of the courtiers were startled at his frankness. 'If I am not to tell the truth to my Sovereign,' replied Buller, 'I don't know to whom I am to tell it.'

[1] At this period the veldt swarmed with herds of deer. 'I have,' says Buller, in a letter written at this time, 'two most charming pets, black greyhounds, who sleep in my bed and keep me warm all night, and are generally cheerful and charming during the day. I had great fun at Kokstadt coursing bucks. I never succeeded in catching one, but we had some wonderful runs, and I got a most wonderful "purl," for poor old "Bob" put his foot in a hole and turned a complete somersault over me. They all thought I must be killed, but by some happy luck I was not hurt in the

least; neither, I am glad to say, was Bob.'

[2] The appointment of A.D.C. to the Sovereign carries with it the rank of full colonel.

Eight – The 2nd Battalion

Colonel Buller had not been long at home when he was posted to the 2nd Battalion, at that time engaged in the Afghan War. His baggage had actually been sent on by ship, and he was on the point of starting in person when stopped by peremptory orders from the Duke of Cambridge. His position as a captain and brevet-colonel would certainly have been anomalous, and might perhaps have resulted in his commanding a company and a brigade on alternate days.

During the early part of 1880 a General Election was evidently at hand, and Redvers Buller was invited to stand in the Liberal interest for North Devon. As to his political views he always called himself an old Whig, but it may be doubted whether the description was accurate. Buller, in his love of the people, was a Tory in the highest sense of the word; in his keenness for reform he was a Radical. In view of his immense local popularity his election was assured, but the Colonel frankly said he could not support Mr. Gladstone on all questions, and the project consequently dropped. That he would have been a force in the House of Commons cannot reasonably be doubted, for he had a wonderful power of converting men to his own views.

After a few months of Staff service in the North British district, Colonel Buller was appointed Assistant Adjutant-General at Aldershot, the command at that time being held by Sir Thomas Steele. During the summer he attended the manoeuvres of the German army. But service in the field was once more at hand. The Zulu War had freed the Boers from danger on the part of the blacks, and they once more demanded their independence. On the refusal of the

British Government they took up arms, and after taking in ambush a British regiment at Bronkhurst Spruit, crossed the frontier and occupied Laing's Nek in the British Colony of Natal. Sir George Colley marched against them with a couple of battalions, his whole available force; but in January 1881 was repulsed in an attempt to storm the strong position. Several British garrisons in the Transvaal had been already beleaguered, and matters became serious. Reinforcements were sent out. The Staff was increased. Sir Evelyn Wood went out as a Brigadier-General, and in February Buller left England to take up the duties of Deputy Adjutant-General. He reached Cape Town on the 26th, and received next day from Wood the startling news that Colley had been killed and his troops defeated at Majuba. But long before he could join General Wood at Newcastle in Natal hostilities had ceased. The following extract from a local newspaper describes his departure from Pietermaritzburg: —

'Yesterday morning the dispatch of a Newcastle mail from the Post Office was an object of unusual interest, to judge by the rapidly gathering throng of spectators who crowded on the Post Office steps, leaned against the rails, or loafed around the buildings. There were two military passengers standing by, upon one of whom all eyes were turned. A tall, muscular, wiry-looking man, with bronzed face and grizzly beard, clad in the ordinary dark blue service tunic — the left breast of which blazed with bright-coloured medal ribbons — drab cord breeches and yellow leather boots, helmet on head, and grasping a serviceable-looking sword. This was Colonel Buller, the Devonshire soldier, the hero of Zlobane, Kambula, and Ulundi, General Wood's right-hand man, the crack commander of cavalry irregulars, a brave officer, a true gentleman, and one who won the esteem and respectful admiration of those whom he commanded and those who knew him only by reputation.'

On reaching Newcastle, Evelyn Wood and Buller went to Laing's Nek to review the Boer army, being received by a guard of honour, composed of Boers who had served under Buller's command during the Zulu War as troopers in the Frontier Light Horse.

Duties of civil administration compelled General Wood to hand over military affairs entirely to Buller, who, at the end of March, was granted the local rank of Major-General. Headquarters were at Newcastle, and a fine force, amounting to some 14,000 men, including our 2nd and 3rd Battalions, was assembled partly at that town, partly at Estcourt, and partly at the advanced post of Mount Prospect. The Boers declared that Butter's arrival was the equivalent of a reinforcement of 10,000 men to the British Army. The two Generals worked out a scheme for the attack of Laing's Nek from the east, which was considered absolutely certain of success, and justified Wood in saying that he held the Boers in the hollow of his hand. Butter's powers of command and administration were conspicuous. His A.D.C., Captain Donald Browne, remarked to the writer that, old friend as he was of the General, he had had up to that time no notion of the extent of his capacity. The Headquarter Staff was largely composed of Riflemen. In addition to the General and his A.D.C., Colonel — now Lord — Grenfell was Chief of the Staff, and Major — now Sir Ronald — Lane was Deputy Adjutant-General. Some few who read this will perhaps remember the cheery meetings between our 2nd and 3rd Battalions; the former commanded by Colonel Algar, the latter by our present Colonel-Commandant, Sir Cromer Ashburnham; the first at Mount Prospect, the second at Bennett's Drift. Near Mount Prospect was also another of our Colonels-Commandant, viz. Sir Edward Hutton, at that time a captain in command of a company of mounted infantry. [1]

The year wore on, and though more than once the peace seemed likely to be broken (for the Boers were stubborn and a party in our Cabinet seemed ready to drive them to extremities), matters settled down and hostilities were never resumed. Buller was glad, for he thought the Boers had been badly treated in 1877. At the same time, he strongly disapproved of the way in which quasi-independence was now given back to them, and his letters give a remarkable prophecy that a very much more serious war, in which we should be confronted with both Free State and Transvaal, would break out before many years had elapsed.

[1] The writer recalls an incident of the period perhaps not entirely devoid of interest. With Captain F. W. Archer and Captain M. C. Boyle he went for a shooting expedition along" the Buffalo river. Transport was hard to get, and General Buller very kindly lent us a team of army mules, telling us to take the greatest care of them. So we did, but one mule was weakly from the outset. After a few days we returned towards Newcastle: the mule got worse and worse, and one evening just before reaching the town, the driver reported its death. We were much annoyed, and so, we knew, would be the General. In the morning, in accordance with his regulation, we sent the driver to cut off its foot; but by this time the mule had happily come to life again. When the General heard the story he was much pleased that the *raison d'etre* of his order had been so clearly proved.

Nine – Egypt, 1882

Returning to England in December, Buller had a short period of rest. In the following year he married Lady Audrey, widow of the Hon. Greville Howard of Castle Rising; but from his wedding tour, hardly begun, he was called away to a new scene of action. Matters in Egypt had long been going from bad to worse, and England found herself at length compelled to intervene and protect the Khedive against his mutinous army, commanded by Arabi Pasha. After the naval bombardment of Alexandria in July, a British Army Corps, under command of Sir Garnet Wolseley, was dispatched to restore order. Wolseley, remembering Buller's services as Head of the Intelligence Department in Ashanti, gave him the same appointment on the present occasion. Buller arrived on the scene only on the 5th September and took up his duties. Night after night he reconnoitred the enemy's position at Tel-el-Kebir. On one occasion he got in rear of the Egyptian lines as far as El-Keraim. On another he sketched them at short range. Reconnoitring so far on the flank and rear, he seems to have had difficulty in observing well the ground in front of the earthworks. To his great annoyance he found, as the army was marching by night to the assault of the lines, that he had failed to see a lunette some few hundreds of yards in front of the entrenchments. Happily the garrison was surprised sleeping. He was present at Arabi's crushing defeat on the 13th, and, having been mentioned in dispatches, received the K.C.M.G. from the Queen and Third Class of the Osmanieh from the Khedive.

Buller returned home. The Egyptian difficulty seemed to be over. It had in truth only just begun. In the following year — 1883 — an Egyptian force, commanded by Hicks Pasha, an Englishman, was literally annihilated at El-Obeid in Darfur by a force of Dervishes from Upper Egypt under the 'Mahdi,' who presently proceeded to threaten the Lower Provinces. In the first days of February 1884 Buller was dispatched to Egypt as second in command to General Graham, who commanded the British garrison at Cairo. Advancing from the port of Trinkitat on the Nubian Coast, Graham encountered the Dervishes at El-Teb, where Baker Pasha had been defeated a few months previously. During the action a gap was made in the firing line, but, under a heavy fire, Sir Redvers, in the quietest way possible, as if on a field day, filled up the gap with a wing of our 3rd Battalion from the reserve. After the action an alarm arose that the enemy was about to attack again, but, in the same quiet way, Buller took the necessary measures of precaution.

A second fight took place a few days later at Tamai. The troops were formed in two squares, one commanded by Graham in person, the other by Sir Redvers. Graham's square became broken, and during the consequent confusion some of its men poured a volley into that of Buller, causing one face to run in. Sir Redvers at once rode outside the square, and with great coolness rallied his men. It was a dramatic incident. By restoring the formation he undoubtedly staved off a terrible disaster, for had his square been really broken, nothing could have saved the army. Then, with his immediate command in good order, well in hand and cleverly posted, his fire, brought to bear in aid of Graham, checked the enemy and saved the situation for that General also. The fight, however, continued to be keen. Noticing that some of his young soldiers were slightly flinching, Buller brought up a gun into line with them and restored their confidence. The conspicuous coolness and generalship of Sir Redvers inspired every officer and man under his command with confidence, and their admiration was increased when, on burning a village next day, they saw him sitting on his horse while bullets were bespattering the rocks all round, utterly ignoring the danger, though all around him were lying flat on the ground. For his 'distinguished services' in this brief campaign he was promoted to the rank of Major-General.

The interval of rest which followed was of short duration. The celebrated General Charles Gordon was by this time beleaguered in Khartoum. To the expedition under Lord Wolseley, sent in the summer of the same year to rescue him, Sir Redvers Buller was appointed Chief of the Staff. Progress up the Nile, even with the aid of Canadian voyageurs specially engaged for the occasion, was slow; Gordon was *in extremis*, and, as a last resource, Lord Wolseley, from Korti, dispatched a column under Sir Herbert Stewart straight across the desert to strike the Nile again at Metammeh, and throw at all events temporary relief into Khartoum. The column reached the Nile. Sir C. Wilson and Lord C. Beresford embarked on board the steamers sent down by Gordon, but on nearing Khartoum found the General dead and the town captured. They consequently rejoined the column. Sir H. Stewart, fatally wounded a few days earlier, shortly afterwards breathed his last; but on hearing of Stewart's wound, Lord Wolseley had at once dispatched his Chief of Staff to take command of the column. Its initial organisation had been criticised by the latter. Its morale was now shaken, and matters were in a condition of chaos surpassing belief, but the arrival of Buller with the Royal Irish Regiment, on the 11th February 1885, restored the confidence of all ranks. Numerical weakness made retreat, however, inevitable. On the 14th the march was begun. The line of retreat ran under the walls of Metammeh. The moment was critical, for a sortie from its gates was imminent, and a large force of Dervishes was known to be approaching from Khartoum. Buller remained with the rearguard. A camel upset its load. Without showing the slightest anxiety or even annoyance, he gave the word to halt, pointed out a better mode of fastening the burden, waited quietly to see it done, and marched on. 'Here is a man we can trust,' was the comment of the baggage guard. The wells of Abu Klea were reached at midday on the 15th. The column was for a short time harassed by 'sniping' on the part of the Arabs, which produced no great effect, but Sir Redvers was struck by a spent bullet, and his A.D.C., Lord Frederick Fitz Gerald, remonstrated with him for exposing himself at such a crisis. His fall at that moment would probably have meant the destruction of the whole column. In the hope of procuring camels the retreat was not resumed till the 23rd, on which day the force from Khartoum, some 10,000 strong, though probably not entirely composed of fighting men, made its appearance. The British column retired at dusk through a defile where a few men posted on either side might have annihilated the force. But everything had been foreseen; nothing forgotten by the General who, during that anxious night inarch, was everywhere. Yet even to his A.D.C. he would not admit the peril, and it was only to the Bishop of Nottingham — better known as Father Brindle, a man loved and respected by the whole force — that at its close he exclaimed: 'Father, I thank God we have got safely out of that.' By a clever ruse next day the enemy was thoroughly deceived and frightened, and though an occasional false alarm occurred, the march was not again molested and Korti was regained in safety. But no one appreciated the feat of arms more than Lord Wolseley, who had awaited the return of the column with the greatest anxiety. This retreat is considered one of Sir Redvers' finest achievements.

For seven years Sir Redvers had been, with little intermission, on active service. He had proved himself a skilful general in the field, though he had not, except for a short period, commanded any large body of men. As a second in command, whether in Zululand, at Tamai, or in the desert, Sir Redvers had shown himself unsurpassed, and although his opportunities of separate command had not been frequent, they had given him the chance of showing his mettle.

Ten - Ireland

The seven years of war were now to be succeeded by fourteen of peace. On the General's return to England he was made Deputy Adjutant-General at Headquarters, but was shortly afterwards called to a different sphere of action. Affairs in Ireland needed a strong hand. In August 1886 Buller was sent there to reorganise the Constabulary, which was at the time somewhat dispirited by a period of hard and anxious work extending over several years. The magnetism of his sympathetic nature evoked warm response. His bluff, outspoken manner, his unvarying cheerfulness and sense of humour, above all his appreciation of hard work loyally performed, encouraged the men to persevere and stopped depression in cases of failure. His power was soon felt throughout the police; he infused new spirit into the men under his command, was always ready to take responsibility, made allowance for failure, and revived the weary forces of law and order.

'Within a single fortnight they had all rallied round him,' says Mr. Gosse, 'and one man expressed the general feeling in declaring "there is not a policeman in the comity of Kerry who would not lay down his life for Sir Redvers."'

This immediate task done, Sir Redvers, at the end of the year, was made Under-Secretary for Ireland. He was now less in his element.

Not that administration was unsuited to his powers. On the contrary, administration — as in the case of so many good soldiers — was probably his strong point. But he had no knowledge of Ireland and did not understand the ways of the Irish. The sense of justice, which was perhaps his most prominent characteristic, became therefore to some extent wasted. It is of course absurd to suppose that the man who mastered the history and peculiarities of the native tribes on the Gold Coast was unaware of the essential difference between land tenure in England and land tenure in Ireland, or of the difference in weights and measures. He had also associated with plenty of Celts in Devonshire, and knew that, partly from desire to please, partly from inaccuracy of mind, exactitude of speech is not always to be found among the race; but his logical mind failed to grasp the fact that in Ireland two and two may make three; more probably, five; but rarely, if ever, four. His conclusions were consequently at times made rather too rapidly; and his opinions, perhaps too openly expressed, elicited strong criticism. His sympathy with the Irish peasantry caused him to be spoken of as a Radical Home Ruler. The report was quite untrue. Sir Redvers never swerved from his Unionist principles, but his views probably differed a good deal from those of the Government which he was serving, and it is possible that his independence of view was remembered to his disadvantage in later days. Although he did a great deal of good work, and the Dublin Castle officials said they had never met his match in the transaction of business, it can hardly be said that his success as Under-Secretary was as great as it had been in reorganising the police.

In October 1887 the General returned to military duty as Quartermaster-General to the Forces. He was not yet forty-eight. His rise during the last nine years had been astonishingly rapid. With the single exception of Lord Wolseley, he was looked on as the ablest man in the Army.

For three years he remained Quartermaster-General. On the 1st October 1890 Sir Redvers was appointed Adjutant-General in succession to Lord Wolseley, a distinction unprecedented for a Major-General, and it is no unkindness to say that the change was welcomed by the Commander-in-Chief, H.R.H. the Duke of Cambridge, with whom he was a prime favourite. He is pronounced by a competent judge to have been the best Adjutant-General that ever ruled at the War Office. His tenure of the appointment was marked by an administrative reform of the first importance, the reorganisation of the Supply and Transport of the Army.

'The status of a non-combatant and relatively insignificant department,' says a distinguished officer, 'was raised to that of one of the most important branches of the administrative staff of the Army. By this change — only possible from the strong personality of its author — by raising its emoluments and by improving the professional prospects of its members, Sir Redvers succeeded in attracting to this previously unpopular Service many of the ablest officers from the ranks of the executive branches of the Army and from the Staff College. A new spirit was thus infused into the administration of this most important department, to the lasting benefit of the British Army. It is generally acknowledged that the supply and transport services of an army, under abnormally trying conditions, have never been more successfully carried out than in the late South African War (1899-1902), and the result of this great achievement is largely due to the metamorphosis effected by Sir Redvers in the reorganisation of the Army Service Corps.

'It is not too much to say that throughout the whole of his career as Adjutant-General, the traces of his early training under Colonel Hawley were plainly to be discerned. The adoption of a more elastic system of infantry drill and tactics, the improvements effected in the discipline of the soldier by a more intelligent treatment, and the betterment of the soldier's life in barracks, were the result of the principles learnt as a young man from the methods and teaching of his old preceptor, Colonel Hawley, deepened and enlarged by his own peculiarly sympathetic nature.'

As Adjutant-General Buller's innate sense of justice vindicated his action on a particularly difficult occasion; and his judicial turn of mind and practical wisdom were the subject of notice by his legal colleagues in a committee appointed to revise the 'Manual of Military Law.' 'I was greatly impressed by his powerful personality,' writes one of them. 'He struck me as a born leader of men, to be obeyed and followed without hesitation, and as being furthermore endowed with a penetrating and shrewd judgment. In short, I do not remember ever meeting any man who made on me such a rapid and strong impression, which further knowledge of him only strengthened. In the transaction of business he was admirable; clear-sighted, firm and reasonable; he knew exactly what he wanted, though he was quite prepared to take less if the House of Commons was not disposed to legislate to the full extent of his views, i.e. for increasing the powers of commanding officers.' ... The report of the Committee...was unanimously adopted.

In his dealings with the Government his homely satire would occasionally come out. A project for an expedition to be fitted out against French encroachment in Nigeria was under discussion, and the Adjutant-General was asked of what the expedition should consist. Convinced that nothing was to be dreaded from men who, if encountered, would be found overcome by malarial fever, his reply was, 'It had better consist of a doctor with a bottle of brandy,' an answer the common sense of which was undeniable, even if not quite appreciated by the august body to whom it was addressed!

In 1891 Sir Redvers became Lieutenant-General. In 1893 he was offered the Command-in-Chief in India *vice* Lord Roberts, then returning home after his long and distinguished career. Looking at the matter purely from the point of view of Sir Redvers' personal career, it seems unfortunate that he should have declined this compliment. It was time for him to be in the saddle once more. The Indian command would have afforded ample scope for his energy, and would have released him from the slavery of the desk.

Two years passed, and then occurred an episode in Sir Redvers' life which has sometimes been incorrectly narrated. The time for the Duke of Cambridge's retirement was evidently at hand. Buller was asked, nay pressed, to succeed H.R.H. as Commander-in-Chief. To anyone with a less keen sense of duty the prospect would have been dazzling in the extreme. Sir Redvers, however, declined, because he looked on Lord Wolseley as being a better man than himself, and would not be a party to superseding him. But the Government of that day refused to nominate Lord "Wolseley. It was, however, obviously too weak to last long. Buller, therefore, procrastinated on the chance of its fall, and in the hope that a new Government would appoint the man whom he thought most fit. And this actually happened, although only just in time, for the Commission appointing Sir Redvers Commander-in-Chief was ready when the defeat of the Government caused its resignation, and the new Premier at once appointed Lord Wolseley. In high circles Buller's self-denial was well known and appreciated. 'I congratulate you on not being Commander-in-Chief,' wrote an old friend at Court. 'The part you are known to have played in the matter is better than any Commander-in-Chief-ship in the world, and in the long run will, I hope, bring you infinitely more satisfaction.' And the Queen remarked to him that though he had declined to be a Commander-in-Chief, he had made one.

Under Lord Wolseley, Sir Redvers continued to serve as Adjutant-General until the expiration of his term of office in September 1897. To the country at large, and to the Army in particular, the advantage gained by his long term of office work was enormous. Anomalies had disappeared, abuses had been reformed. His untiring industry and talent had never been more conspicuously displayed; but to the General himself the desk was less advantageous. Circumstances had increased the labour of the Adjutant-General almost beyond human power of endurance, and his grey hair betrayed the strain of the hard work which he had undergone. But if he was no longer in all respects the Buller of 1885, it must be remembered that the wear and tear had entirely been incurred in his country's service. Events were shortly to prove that his powers of endurance were unabated; but he was no longer a young man, and thirteen years had elapsed since his last personal command of troops. In the summer of 1898 manoeuvres took place on an extended scale. They are chiefly notable for the fact that they gave Sir Redvers, who commanded one side, the chance of noticing the work done by Colonel French, the result being that twelve months later French was appointed to the command of the Cavalry Division in South Africa with the rank of Lieutenant-General. In the following October Sir Redvers took up the command at Aldershot. Both with officers and men he was very popular. He harassed no one, yet imparted a great deal of quiet instruction to the Division at large and to his own Staff in particular, his object being to encourage independent thought and initiative among the junior officers, and even among the rank and file.

Eleven - Aldershot

During the spring and summer of 1899 it became more and more obvious that war with the South African Republic could hardly be averted. In the month of June Sir Redvers was informed that he had been selected as Commander-in-Chief in the event of hostilities. Sir Redvers pointed out that any force of less than 50,000 men would be inadequate, even setting aside the certainty that the Orange Free State would have to be reckoned with in addition to the Transvaal, and that the only practicable line of attack was through the Free State. Discussion either of this route or of any question connected with the attitude of the Free State was, however, declined; and a little later on the suggestions made by the General for strengthening the garrisons of Cape Colony and Natal were disregarded. It was not until the 29th September that the route through the Orange Free State, advocated by Sir Redvers, was sanctioned by the Government, and that preparations for the march of the army could be made at the ports of disembarkation. In regard to calling out the reserves, and in the date for his own departure, the Government was unable to accede to Sir Redvers' urgent requests; and in spite of the untiring zeal and ability of General Sir H. Brackenbury, Master-General of the Ordnance, the time lost by the failure to make the necessary preparations in advance could never afterwards be entirely made up. Sir Redvers asked that his old friend, Lieut.-General Sir Francis Grenfell, who had great experience of South Africa and had served with him during the Kaffir and Zulu wars as well as in 1881, might go out as second in command; but Sir Francis, being the Governor of Malta, and employed in an important political office, could not be spared by the Colonial Office. It was, nevertheless, unfortunate that Buller should have been without the assistance of any of his old companions in arms.

On the 14th of October Sir Redvers left London and embarked at Southampton amid a scene of enthusiasm never to be forgotten by anyone present. But, pleased as he could not fail to be by the demonstration, Buller by no means shared the sanguine views of the country at large. He knew the theatre of war too well to ignore the fact that the geographical area, strength, and political conditions of South Africa made his task a gigantic one. On the voyage he remarked to a friend that the business was too great for one man, and predicted that Lord Roberts would be sent out after him.

His ship arrived at Cape Town on the evening of the 30th, and Sir Redvers was met with news the like of which, it is possible, has never in the world's history been received by a Commander-in-Chief on reaching his base of operations. The force of 15,000 men appointed to defend Southern Natal was practically surrounded in Lady smith. The whole colony, the capital, even the seaport town of Durban, lay at the mercy of the Boers. There was no available cavalry; it was shut up in Lady smith. His Chief of the Staff and many other members of it could not join the General; they were shut up in Ladysmith. In the Cape Colony things were not much better. The

Boers were already occupying the northern side, and were being joined every day by hundreds of rebel colonists. There was no force to stop them. Cape Town itself was seething with disaffection. It almost seemed as if the British flag might disappear from South Africa before troops could arrive from home. The duty allotted to the General on leaving England had been a punitive expedition into the Transvaal; that which he had now before him involved, in addition, the recovery of a great part of our own Colonies.

'There are,' said Sir Edward Grey in Parliament at a later date, 'people who, reflecting on the history of the war, say that, bad as things were at first, they were as nothing to what it would have been had the Boers . . . made a rush for Cape Town. Sir Redvers had to face that situation, and he had an almost impossible task.'

Overweighted by this gigantic problem, but with firm heart and strong resolve, Buller at once set himself to work. Feeling it impossible, at a distance of 1000 miles, to interfere with an experienced and responsible officer, he contented himself, like Napoleon with Moreau in 1800, by indicating his views to the General in Natal, without insisting on them. One thing only he positively ordered, viz. that General French, appointed to command the British cavalry — and, with the exception of his personal staff, the only officer appointed at Sir Redvers' own instance — should be allowed to quit Ladysmith and join him. The General's activity during the next ten days was everywhere conspicuous, and infused a new spirit into everyone with whom he came in contact. 'On arrival at Cape Town,' says an officer, 'we found everybody in a rather demoralised condition. It was wonderful to see the way in which Sir Redvers restored confidence all round. By the time we left the Cape for Natal he had induced all the authorities to take quite a cheerful view of the situation.' Colonial mounted infantry were raised on the lines of his old corps, the Frontier Light Horse. [1] Transport was organised; martial law, where necessary, proclaimed; the small forces available — one regiment of cavalry, three batteries Royal Artillery, three and a half battalions infantry — posted to the best advantage. But affairs in Natal cried urgently for relief. To save the port of Durban was a matter of supreme importance. Four Brigades, as they arrived from England, were sent on thither, although Buller's whole plan of campaign — an advance through the Orange Free State — was dislocated thereby. He soon found his own presence in Natal indispensable, and landed at Durban on the 25th November. His reinforcements had been just in time to save Maritzburg. On their advance the tide of invasion was checked, and rolled back behind the Tugela.

The subsequent events of the campaign are too recent to enable us to see them in their true perspective, and this is not the place either to narrate them in detail or to enter into controversy. [2] Sufficient then to say, that Southern Natal being cleared, the relief of Ladysmith became Sir Redvers' next objective. The Boers remembered him of old. 'I have to tell you,' said the Boer General, Joubert, to his army, 'that we now have to face the bravest and finest general in the world, who is accompanied by an army of men who would go through fire and water for him. To those of you who fought in the previous struggle with the English I need not say that I speak of General Buller.'

But the problem before the British commander was one to test the powers of a Wellington. In front of him, covered by an unfordable river, was the position of the enemy, described as c a series of natural Gibraltars strengthened by the best military science.' The Boer trenches were novel in character, and were connected by pathways cleared of all stones, so that inter-communication was easy. The Boers, being invisible all the time, were able to move laterally through the trenches without being seen. 'The British Army,' said the late Sir Howard Vincent at the Royal United Service Institute, 'lay upon a plain, its every movement under the eyes of the enemy, securely hidden in the mountain fastnesses of the further shore. Not all the engineers of the armies of Europe could have improved upon that work of Nature. No description which I have read of the task approached the reality. A less persistent and less enduring soldier than Sir Redvers Buller would have renounced it as hopeless.' An officer who took a prominent part in the action had occasion to visit the ground some three years afterwards. His idea was that he would find it incredible that the correct solution of the task had not been discovered at a glance, but upon reaching the spot the problem appeared more insoluble than ever. What surprised him was, not that there had been failures, but that there had ever been ultimate success.

Buller was under no delusion. He had truly described the undertaking as a forlorn hope, and for that reason was going to lead it in person. The plan was to dispatch a force of Colonial troops through Zululand to occupy a position near Helpmakaar, some miles east of the besieged town, while with the bulk of his army he crossed the Tugela at Potgeiter's Drift and approached Ladysmith from the south-west. But now came the news of Gatacre's misfortune at Stormberg and Lord Methuen's failure at Magersfontein; and Sir Redvers felt that a flank march of fifty miles to Potgeiter's Drift in the face of an enemy elated by the success of its comrades was no longer justifiable. He therefore decided to effect a lodgment on the farther bank of the Tugela by Colenso, after which he felt convinced that a combined attack by his own army in front and by the Ladysmith garrison in rear would infallibly cause the Boers to evacuate their position. In communicating this decision to the Secretary of State on the 13th December the General, however, added, that in the event either of success or failure it would then become necessary to stand for a time on the defensive, with a view to the organisation and training of mobile troops. He also pointed out that in any event it must be understood that the defence of Southern Natal, and not the relief of Ladysmith, must be his primary object. Students of military history will remember that in 1810 Wellington advanced for the avowed object of relieving Ciudad Rodrigo; yet allowed the fortress to fall under his very eyes, because he found himself too weak for the task and was not going to risk his primary object — the defence of Portugal.

Sir Redvers now prepared to face the passage of the Tugela. An alternative line of advance by his right against the Hlangwane mountain presented itself; but the heights were covered by thick scrub, and to expose therein troops not inured to bush fighting seemed hazardous. This line also involved a departure from those roads indicated by his friends in Ladysmith as best suited to their co-operation.

Early on the morning of the 15th the troops advanced to the attack. The circumstances which caused it to be broken off are well known and need not be alluded to here. The point that concerns us is that the confidence of the troops in their commander remained quite unshaken. Hearing almost at the outset that two batteries were gravely compromised, Buller hastened to the spot, but his utmost efforts failed to rescue more than two of the guns. Sitting on his horse under a heavy fire, he was struck by the splinter of a shell. The abandonment of the remaining ten guns was the subject of the sharpest criticism subsequently directed against the General. Whether the guns could or could not have been saved must always remain a matter of opinion. It should, however, be observed that Sir Redvers' decision is supported by men who had the best means of forming an opinion, and was, at all events, that of a strong, not of a weak man. No one better than himself could foresee the acrimony with which his conduct would be assailed. But, rightly or wrongly — whether bearing in mind or forgetting Napoleon's maxim that in war the moral is to the physical as three to one — Buller judged that the lives of his men were more precious than guns. He decided to sacrifice the guns rather than to further sacrifice his troops. In his annoyance and in the pain of his wound he may have used loose expressions, such as that the guns could easily be replaced; but the thought that he was to be the first British general for nearly a century to incur the stigma of losing guns must to him have been anguish beyond power of words to express. By the intense heat of the day, by the contusion which he had received, by the strain and disappointment which he had undergone, even Buller's iron frame was exhausted. Having withdrawn his troops, he telegraphed without reservation to the Secretary of State the result of the action. He added a sentence reviewing the situation and asking for Ministerial opinion on the political question. The point of this telegram was misunderstood. Field-Marshal Lord Roberts was appointed to the supreme command in South Africa, while Buller's command was henceforward to be confined to Natal. The latter cheerfully acquiesced in the decision, for he had long been convinced that it was impossible for one man to conduct two lines of military operations 1000 miles apart; but, alluding to this in his diary, H.R.H. the Duke of Cambridge remarks: 'It strikes every old soldier, including myself, that this is very hard measure to Buller, who has had enormous difficulties to contend with thus far, owing to the want of news and to the bad preparations before his arrival in the field.' Next morning a heliogram was sent to Sir George White in Lady smith, the purport of which has also been strangely misapprehended. Suffice it to say, that in the whole British Empire there was no one less likely to suggest the surrender of a fortified position than Sir Redvers Buller.

The situation was correctly and graphically described by Dr. Miller Maguire, the well-known authority on military history, in the *Morning Post*:

On the date when this disputed message was sent to Sir G. White the supreme command in South Africa was in Sir Redvers Buller's hands, as Lord Roberts did not arrive at Cape Town till some weeks later. But at that time our strategy was unquestionably affected and spoiled by political considerations. Our army for these reasons was split up into three parts — disconnected and incapable of reciprocal support. The General in command must have known of the dangers of this course, at least as well as any critic. He retained the largest portion under himself at Colenso, Lord Methuen had the next largest at Modder River, and the third fraction, under General Gatacre, was at or near Stormberg. In addition to these troops, Sir George White with the remnant of his 10,000 men was shut up in Ladysmith.

Without going into figures, anyone with any military knowledge would at once recognise that the troops under Sir Redvers' command were much too few to even watch the immense frontier line he set himself to protect. From subsequent events, including the necessity for the recent proclamation of Martial Law in Cape Colony, there can now be no reasonable doubt but that, had he not guarded that frontier line, Natal and Cape Colony would both have been temporarily lost to the British Crown, and only been reoccupied at a great expenditure of lives and money before it would be possible to undertake the subsequent conquest of the Orange Free State and Transvaal. Therefore, on the 16th December 1899, the problem before the General in command in South Africa was this: — 'I have a very long frontier line which I must guard, otherwise these Colonies will be lost to the Crown, at any rate "pro tem.," and I have nothing like enough troops to do this effectively. But there is Ladysmith and its garrison. I have made an unsuccessful attempt to relieve it; if I try again I must certainly lose another 2000 or 3000 men, probably more, and if I fail a second time, the Boers will certainly invade Natal and I will not then be strong enough to stop them. If Ladysmith falls it will be a great disaster, but quite an insignificant one compared with the loss of the two Colonies. Therefore of the two evils I choose the lesser, and I had better make up my own mind and see that the Commander in Ladysmith understands what I think he should do in case his provisions give out before I am in a position to again make a forward movement for his relief.' Will anyone say that this was not a prudent arrangement on the part of a commander? His accusers have not even hinted that Sir Redvers ever contemplated the possibility of his own Army surrendering. The garrison of Ladysmith was not conducting an active defence, and was of little value in preventing a Boer invasion of Natal. No doubt there was a great deal of sentiment about the relief of Ladysmith, but 'sentiment' is not 'war.' On the assumption, therefore, that Sir Redvers sent Sir George White certain suggestions as to what he should do in case his supplies gave out before he could have been relieved, can any critic prove that this was not a perfectly prudent forethought, more especially as the message should have been known to no one except to Sir George and his confidential Staff-Officer? When the full history of the campaign is written, will anyone suggest that, from a strategical point of view, Sir R. Buller was quite wrong, under any circumstances, in making up his mind to let Ladysmith fall, if necessary, in preference to increasing the risk of losing the Colonies of Natal and the Cape, disasters which would have probably included the loss of Methuen's and Gatacre's columns, and perhaps all his own guns and train?

The truth is, we have been involved in all these difficulties because, though we had a few thousand soldiers, not nearly enough for any real war, we had no organisation worthy of the name of Army in 1899, and the governing classes neither knew nor cared about what war meant. They were so accustomed to cheap victories over badly armed and naked savages, or over semi-civilised communities, which had long been accustomed to conquerors, that they could not comprehend the difficulties of Generals in real warfare with a fair match. Not one official in ten, civil or military, had taken the pains to study in any text-book or general treatise like Bloch's the probable tactical effects of magazines and smokeless powder. Unless these folks change their system forthwith, the South African disasters are only preliminaries to utter ruin. It is said that if Ladysmith had fallen 'the Empire would have been shaken to pieces.' The fall of Strasburg did not shake France to pieces; the fall of Sebastopol did not shake Russia to pieces; the fall of New Orleans did not shake the Confederacy to pieces. If the temporary fall of Ladysmith would have been disastrous, the Empire must now have for citizens a very feeble generation. Had the Boers been Frenchmen or Germans, it would assuredly have fallen. Indeed, the foreign friends of the Boers say that these proved their utter incapacity by not isolating it and keeping it isolated permanently, in spite of both White and Buller, once White was shut in.

It is not at all bad strategy to abandon territory 'pro tem.,' and to let a fortress or two go is often good strategy.

And now Buller turned his thoughts to his first project. Crossing the Tugela at Potgeiter's Drift, he hoped, with the bulk of his army, to envelop the Boer right, and when their centre should be weakened by reinforcing the threatened flank, to break through it with a selected brigade. The conception of the plan is admitted by all to have been good. Its execution failed. But to us of the 60th the fight is interesting from the fact that, according to the admission of Botha's Chief of the Staff, the seizure of the Twin Peaks by our 3rd

Battalion actually pierced the enemy's line, threatened his right, and forced his left to retire. It was impossible to feed the Battalion, and it was recalled. During the night of January 24th the hill of Spion Kop was unfortunately evacuated. When day dawned it looked as if the army would be hurled back into the Tugela. But the danger merely served to sharpen the General's faculties. It was when others despaired that Buller was at his best and coolest. The situation, and what followed, is graphically described by Mr. Winston Churchill. 'The enemy was flushed with success. The opposing lines were in many places scarcely 1000 yards apart. As the infantry retired, the enemy would have commanding ground from which to assail them at every point. Behind flowed the Tugela, a deep, rapid, only occasionally fordable river, 85 yards broad, with precipitous banks. We all prepared ourselves for a bloody and even disastrous rearguard action. But now, I repeat, when things had come to this pass, Buller took personal command. He arrived on the field calm, cheerful, inscrutable as ever, rode hither and thither with a weary Staff and a huge note-book, gripping the whole business in his strong hands, and so shook it into shape that we crossed the river in safety, comfort, and good order, with most remarkable mechanical precision, and without the loss of a single man or a pound of stores.'

A day or two afterwards General Buller briefly addressed his troops at Spearman's Camp. 'Your gallantry,' said he, 'has given me the key to Ladysmith.' The words were inaudible to the great majority, but the effect was magical. The men knew that their General was pleased with them, and the fact was enough to inspire them with renewed enthusiasm. Then, speaking to the 60th, in reference to their capture of the Twin Peaks, he said. 'I have lost in two of your officers one of my oldest friends and the son of one of my oldest friends. But had God seen fit to give me a son, I should have been proud if he had lost his life the other day with the 3rd Battalion of the 60th Rifles.'

Sir Redvers now made preparations for a third attempt, and a few days later pierced the enemy's line at Vaal Krantz. He was by this time within ten miles of Lady smith. But to drive his advantage home would, he reckoned, cost him from three to four thousand men, and the mountainous country prevented his supporting the infantry with artillery fire. With the full assent of his generals [3] he decided that the attempt was too hazardous, and once more withdrew to the right bank of the Tugela. But he had already decided on a new plan, viz. to turn the left of the enemy's position by the Hlangwane mountain, east of Colenso.

Three times he had been baffled, and to an ordinary man three disappointments might have been fatal to his prestige with the men under his command. But Buller was no ordinary person. His troops would return whistling to their bivouacs (where good meals had already been prepared for them), smarting under no sense of defeat, thinking each movement was only a part of the game, and anxious only to know what 'old Buller' thought of their conduct. In place of being shaken, the men's confidence in their General seemed rather higher than ever. 'They had followed their leader, General Buller,' says Captain Blake Knox, Royal Army Medical Corps, in his admirable account of 'Buller's Campaign,' 'never questioning, never doubting, even through the dark, dark days of Colenso and Spion Kop, and they were prepared to follow him anywhere and at any time. Never was a General more confidently looked up to through adversity than was our Natal chief. He sought it not, but the feeling came spontaneously from every heart. Crippled as he was for want of maps, having for months to face a position impregnable to his force, he never flinched at a check, but resolutely returned for a fresh attack.'

> Men who followed to the death —
> Men who gave their latest breath —
> To cheer and charge for Buller and their country and their Queen.

The administrative system of Buller's army was excellent. His transport arrangements formed the model on which those in our Army at the present day are regulated. His arrangements for the care of the sick and wounded were splendid. At the suggestion of his able Senior Medical Officer, Colonel — now Surgeon-General Sir Thomas — Gallwey, Colonial Bearer Corps to the number of between two and three thousand men were organised, and the diminution of his fighting strength contingent on men leaving the ranks to pick up wounded, was thus avoided. 'He also instituted hospital ships,' says Sir Thomas; 'eventually we had six and a fortnightly service to England. A convalescent Depot of 50 officers and 1500 N.C.O.'s and men was also approved by him. He insisted on the principle of removing our sick and wounded immediately from the fighting force. He approved of a large improvised hospital being moved over to Mount Alice to provide for the engagements at Spion Kop and Vaal Krantz, well provided with female nurses, the first time on record that nurses were admitted so near the scene of action. He was very particular about sites of camps and good feeding, always providing fresh meat and vegetables as soon as troops were disengaged from action. This of course had a favourable bearing on the health of the troops, for during the three and a half months of desperate fighting before the relief of Ladysmith, we had very little sickness, but when we got into the Boer lines and were encamped awaiting orders from Lord Roberts for the further advance northward, we were attacked with enteric, although not to such an extent as was the army on the western side.

'The establishment of Field Force Canteens — so far as I know the first ever established with an army in the field — aided materially in keeping up the health and efficiency of the Army.

'I have personally discussed all these and many other questions with Sir Redvers,' adds the Surgeon-General. 'He took me into his absolute confidence, and the consequence of this, as well as of the advice and invaluable intelligence which he freely gave, was that I was enabled to provide medical arrangements for the Natal Campaign such as had never before been afforded to any army in the field. I saw him at all times, night and day, whenever I required his advice, and what particularly impressed me was, not only the alacrity and clearness of head with which he invariably entered into any proposition, but the marvellous rapidity with which he grasped its essentials. The ideals we aimed at were to keep up our fighting strength by exercising every possible preventive measure against disease, and to procure within reason every care and comfort for our sick and wounded. No army was ever better looked after in these respects.'

And Sir Frederick Treves has remarked of Sir Redvers that 'no hospital was pitched without his entering fully into the matter; all questions of sites were discussed with him; no engagement was commenced without the medical staff getting a message from Headquarters to prepare for the number of cases expected, and General Buller was full of anxiety as to how the sick were to be accommodated.' In an article in the *Nineteenth Century* Sir Frederick also remarks: 'So far as the Natal part of the campaign is concerned, I can speak with gratitude of the continued and most solicitous interest which General Buller took in all matters connected with the sick and wounded, and of his eagerness to make perfect in every way the work of the medical department.'

As regards the devotion and admiration of the men towards their General, a volume might be written.

'*The Majestic,*' writes a journalist, 'arrived on Sunday at Southampton, with 40 officers and 310 men wounded at the front. Nearly all of them had formed part of the Lady smith relief force...Five had lost the use of limbs, and many suffered partial, and one or two total, loss of sight. The men, however, say they would have gone anywhere and done anything for Buller.' 'I am about daily in the hospital,' writes another from Aldershot, 'and have not yet come across a single man out of the 500 or 600 sick and wounded who does not speak in very warm tones indeed of General Buller's wonderful ability and success against fearful difficulties.'

A man of the Fusilier Brigade which had served under Buller up to the relief of Ladysmith and had afterwards been transferred to the army in the Orange River Colony, writing a few months later, says: 'We are all very proud to hear of General Buller's great success in Natal. Everyone who has been fighting under him says he is the best commander they have ever been under. I think he does not get half as much praise as he should, for he was a father to us during the relief of Ladysmith, and I can't wonder the people of Devonshire being so fond of him, for his coolness and presence of mind in every engagement is most extraordinary.'

But further testimony is superfluous. Even the Minister most hostile to Sir Redvers admitted that he never lost the confidence of his troops.

The views of the enemy are, however, interesting. The Boers declared they would have had it all their way but for Buller. They never for a moment thought it possible for him to relieve Ladysmith.

Sir Redvers now returned to the neighbourhood of Colenso. He found the Boers in occupation of the village and of a concave line of heights, following the course and south of the Tugela river. Hussar Hill, forming a sort of outlying bastion, was seized on the 14th February. Cingolo, forming the extreme left of the enemy's line, was captured on the 17th. Monte Christo, immediately north of Cingolo, and Green Hill in advance of it, were taken next day, in spite of the intense heat and the fact that it was almost impossible to provide the troops with water. On the 19th the Hlangwane mountain was occupied, and the enemy driven across the Tugela. On the 21st Buller threw a pontoon bridge across the Tugela, two miles below Colenso, and crossed the river. Next day he seized the lower kopjes on the left bank and made a lodgment on Hedge Hill, above the Onderbrook Spruit. On the 23rd he gained possession of the spurs of Hart's Hill; but, dissatisfied with his progress and fearing that he would capture the crest of Hart's Hill only at terrible cost, he withdrew his army once more to the right bank of the Tugela, cleverly covering his retirement by the advanced brigades on Hart's Hill. An informal armistice to enable the collection of the wounded took place on the 25th. On the 26th Sir Redvers threw his pontoon bridge across the Tugela three miles lower down, opposite Hlangwane, posting his guns on that and on the other hills on the right bank of the Tugela. On the 27th he threw the troops across, captured the heights forming the left of the enemy's position, and rolled up his line. For eleven consecutive days his troops had been under fire. The success of the action of this last day, known as the Battle of Pieter's Hill, was decisive. Lord Dundonald rode into La-dysmith the following evening, and the relief of the town was a *fait accompli.* Being sure that the enemy was out of his reach, Sir Redvers preferred to bring up his supply wagons at once into starv-ing Ladysmith, rather than hinder them by filling up the roads with columns of troops in what would probably be a useless pursuit, and thus disappoint the suffering garrison of its much-needed food.

'Really,' said Sir Redvers in a letter reproduced in facsimile oppo-site, 'the manner in which the men have worked, fought, and en-dured during the last fortnight has been something more than hu-man; broiled in a burning sun by day, drenched in rain by night, ly-ing about three hundred yards off an enemy who shoots you if you show as much as a finger; they could hardly eat or drink by day, and as they were usually attacked by night, they got but little sleep, and through it all were as cheery and willing as could be.'

'Then,' says the talented authoress of 'The Burden of Proof,' 'at last came home the glorious news of the relief of Ladysmith, and the country went wild with acclamation over the bulldog tenacity of this true Englishman and true Devonian, who never knew when he was beaten.'

A Colonial remarked: 'Buller must be made of cast-iron to stand it all. First, there was the one day at Colenso, next five days at Spion Kop, then two days at Krantz Kloof, finally ending up with thirteen days on the Boer left front, culminating in the Battle of Pieter's Sta-tion. This last was a most brilliant and heroic piece of work.'

My dearest -

Here I am at last. I thought I was never going to get here - we have had a hard busy time, and then ...... till .... last ...... I ...... have not had time ...... and sleep much ......

However it is all over a well over thanks God - we began fighting on the 14: February and ...... fought every day and nearly all every night also till the 27th. So we had plenty of it - I must say this men were grand, they meant to do it

2/

and it was a real pleasure to command them — It has all seemed to me like a dream: Every day some new complications to meet and my day the same roar of guns and rattle of muskets, with alas, every day the long list of killed and wounded, which is what I cannot bear — ...... I thought that if I got in it would cost me 3000 men, and I hope I have done it under 2000 which is something.

Congratulations telegrams of all sorts are showing in upon me, and I feel that the great

And finally, writing of both officers and men, a Royal Engineer describes the country thus: 'The theatre of war, both north and south of the Tugela, is like nothing the vast majority of Englishmen hitherto have seen — in fact, in tremendous, intricate, and interminable obstacles, it probably surpasses anything they ever imagined. To realise the unique and fortified mountains that the relieving army had to break through is to accuse Buller's severe critics of an ungenerous impatience in wondering that his methods appeared slow.

'Indeed, it's a marvel he succeeded in forcing his way through a land likened only to a country of "linked Plevnas," bristling with natural fortresses. When the apparent key to a position had been captured, it was found to be commanded by a higher point that was revealed above, but was invisible from below. It is a combination of mountains and almost unassailable positions, with an absolutely invisible enemy. It was a gigantic labyrinth to which there was no known clue, and that labyrinth, as has been shown, was lined with death. The *impasse* must have seemed hopeless. And, of course, the Boers were finally convinced that no human power could break through the barrier they had created between the perishing garrison of Ladysmith and the army under Buller. ... If Buller had abandoned Ladysmith to its fate, the impartial military critic could have only exonerated him from blame. But I am sure the preposition "if" never entered the mind of an Englishman. With every difficulty, with every danger, the higher mounted the courage of our troops... Success was attained, and the almost impossible achieved by a splendid army under a splendid man.'

The hospitals were Sir Redvers' first care on entering Ladysmith. Not the smallest detail escaped him. 'Most officers look round and go out again. *Our* General' — as the men delighted to call him — 'knows at a glance what we want and has it done.' By almost feminine intuition he seemed to realise how to give comfort and relieve pain.

Sir Redvers' telegram, announcing the relief of Ladysmith, created a great impression from its modest wording and extreme simplicity. He issued the following spirited army order to his troops: —

'Soldiers of Natal! The relief of Ladysmith unites two forces, both of which have, during the last few months, striven with conspicuous gallantry and splendid determination to maintain the honour of their Queen and country.

'The garrison of Ladysmith have, during four months, held their position against every attack with complete success, and endured many privations with admirable fortitude.

'The relieving force has had to force its way through an unknown country, across an unfordable river, and over almost inaccessible heights, in the face of a fully prepared, well-armed, and tenacious enemy. By the exhibition of the truest courage — the courage that burns steadily, as well as flashes brilliantly — it has accomplished its object and added a glorious page to the history of the British Empire.

'Ladysmith has been held and is relieved. Sailors and soldiers, Colonials and home-bred, have done this; united by one desire, inspired by one patriotism.

'The General Officer Commanding congratulates both forces upon the martial qualities they have shown; he thanks them for their determined efforts, and he desires to offer his sincere sympathy to the relatives and friends of those good soldiers and gallant comrades who have fallen in the fight.'

Sir Redvers was anxious to lose no time in following up his success, and proposed to force Van Reenan's Pass and occupy Harrismith, but the Commander-in-Chief felt unable to assent, and directed him to remain strictly on the defensive. It was not until the beginning of May that the Natal army was permitted to advance. By this time the Boers, to the number of some 8000, had had ample time to strongly fortify their position on the Biggarsberg. But Buller, moving due east on Helpmakaar, outwitted the enemy, and by a fine combination turned the Biggarsberg on the 13th. The Boers evacuated their strong positions, hotly pursued by Dundonald and his mounted brigade. On the 15th Buller entered Dundee, where he again formed a junction with the 5th Division, which had been advancing northward by the direct Ladysmith — Newcastle road. On the 18th the Union Jack was once more hoisted in Newcastle. The brilliant operations of twelve days had sufficed to clear the enemy out of Northern Natal with the one exception of Laing's Nek. Our losses were almost *nil.*

The territory had been regained by skill, not by brute force, yet no Boers were left behind to sever Sir Redvers' communications. A halt was now necessary to repair the railway and bring up supplies. The Boers occupied the crests of the Drakenberg to the north and east. The problem before the British commander was the penetration of the mountain chain. To force the celebrated Laing's Nek position would obviously entail terrible loss of life. Sir Redvers determined to put into execution a plan which he had resolved on in case of need before leaving England. On the 28th, the railway being repaired as far as Newcastle and a reserve of food collected, Buller, as a feint, menaced the Boer left by means of General Hildyard's Division, sent due east to Utrecht. The next few days were occupied with negotiations between Sir Redvers and the Boer Commandant, Christian Botha. They were broken off on 5th June. The delay was entirely in our favour, facilitating preparations for a further advance. On the same evening, covered by a Division which was occupying a position opposite Laing's Nek, Hildyard, in accordance with Buller's instructions, retraced his steps and, concealed by the darkness, moved due eastward on Botha's Pass, separating Natal from the Orange River Colony. On the 8th he cleverly captured the Pass. On the 9th Buller, who had accompanied Hildyard, resumed the advance beyond the Drakenberg in a northerly direction. On the 11th he found the enemy occupying a strong position at Alleman's Nek in Transvaal territory, some four miles east of Volksrust. By this time Laing's Nek had been completely turned, and it only remained to follow up the advantage. The position was forced after the Boers had sustained a loss, according to their own confession, greater than any other in the course of the war. Buller's casualties were 23 killed and 120 wounded. The action forced the enemy to evacuate Laing's Nek in all haste. This grand operation was perhaps the most ably executed and the most effective of the whole war. On the loth the army concentrated at Volksrust. Standerton was occupied on the 22nd, Heidelburg a few days later.

In a letter describing these operations an officer in a high position on the Staff writes: 'I want to let you know how proud we all are of our commander, and how pleased we all are for his sake at the splendid success with which we have driven the enemy out of the Biggarsberg, Laing's Nek, and Majuba — a success which is entirely due to Sir Redvers' most skilful operations. I must say this because, as no doubt you have seen in his official telegrams, he always gives the credit for each success to his subordinates. But that is just like him, and we all know better; and if it had not been for his masterly dispositions, we should now either be still facing one of the many barriers which we had to get across, or if we had forced it we should have only done so with very heavy loss of valuable life.

'After the relief of Ladysmith...Sir Redvers was directed to occupy the enemy's attention in the Biggarsberg. He did it so successfully that he turned them neck and crop out of it. His flank movement round by Helpmakaar quite deceived the enemy, for, as Commandant Botha's Staff Officer told us, they expected us to force Van Touder's Pass, whereas we seized Helpmakaar before they quite knew what we were up to.

'Interesting as were our operations in the Biggarsberg, they were, I think, quite put in the shade by the turning of Laing's Nek. We found ourselves face to face with the strongest position I have ever seen, held by an enemy who had been reinforced by fresh troops which had come in from in front of Lord Roberts, while on our left was the Drakenberg, of which all the passes were held; but Sir Redvers again entirely outmanoeuvred the enemy, who had signified their intention of holding on to Laing's Nek to the last possible moment. When, however (after a very brilliant action at Alleman's Nek, the success of which was in a great measure due to the fact of Sir Redvers in person placing the guns where they would have the best effect), the enemy found their communications cut, they left Laing's Nek and Majuba as hard as they could go.

'...Of one thing I am quite certain, and that is that there is not a man in the Army who does not realise that we owe our success to Sir Redvers. As I said in the beginning of my letter, we are all proud to serve under him, and would follow him anywhere with the greatest delight, as we *always* have done.'

Sir Redvers was now directed to concentrate his army at Paarde Kop, between Standerton and Volksrust, for the advance northward on Machadodorp in combination with Lord Roberts from Pretoria. Starting on the 7th August he occupied Amersfoort after a stiff engagement. On the 15th Buller reached Twyfelaar, after a march of 100 miles through difficult country. Here he had to wait for the Commander-in-Chief. [4] On the 26th he drove the Boers from some strong positions at Geluk, some ten miles south-east of Belfast. Next day the enemy was found in occupation of a very strong position, with its centre at Bergendal on the Netherlands Railway. The assault of the position was entrusted to Sir Redvers, who carried it out with great ability, captured the heights, and gained a decisive victory. The enemy gave way at all points, flying north and eastward in great confusion. Buller's loss was only about 150 men, the greater part sustained by the Rifle Brigade in a brilliant charge. Lydenburg was reached on the 7th September, after a march through incredibly rough country.

On the 9th Buller, whose force was by this time reduced to Dundonald's Mounted Brigade, a brigade of infantry and three batteries, advanced to the top of the Mauchberg mountain, and came in sight of the whole of Botha's army, but far out of reach of our field guns. On the 11th he went to Spitz Kop and the Sabie Valley, and then to Pilgrim's Rest. On the 1st October he returned to Lydenburg by way of Kruger's Post. There was now no more work for him to do. He gave up the command, and began his journey homeward after speaking a few words of farewell to each unit of his command. 'Each regiment,' says Captain Blake Knox, 'gave him a round of cheers, and surely never was so hearty a cheer given a general. General Buller's progress from Lydenburg to Machadodorp was veritably a triumphant one. Along the line of communication every little post and every garrison turned out to wish him farewell. No stereotyped cheer was there; the hearty welcome that greeted him could only have come from most sincere hearts and throats. One is not surprised, for in the early days of the war Sir Redvers Buller had ever been at hand, ever mindful of his men, sharing their troubles and pleasures alike, though in those days it was mostly trouble. Later, when things went well, the sight of Sir Redvers Buller ever brought back to our minds those days of hard and stern fighting by which he saved Natal.'

On the 10th October Lord Roberts published the following special Army Order: 'General the Right Honourable Sir Redvers Buller, V.C., G.C.B., K.C.M.G., having relinquished the command of the Natal Field Force and being about to return to England, the Field-Marshal Commanding in Chief cannot allow him to leave South Africa without thanking him for the great services he has rendered to his country while in command of that force, as well as for the ability with which he has carried out the operations while serving with the forces under Lord Roberts' immediate command, which have resulted in the collapse of the Boer army in the eastern portion of the Transvaal.' In South Africa his services were most thoroughly realised and appreciated, and met with no grudging acknowledgment. 'General Buller,' observed Sir Walter Peace, Agent-General to Natal, 'saved Natal, saved South Africa, and saved the British Empire.' And at Cape Town at an entertainment in which pictures of popular generals were shown by the cinematograph, and received more or less approval, when the picture of General Buller appeared on the scene the audience went frantic.

It is remarkable that no sooner had the man whom the Boers dreaded gone home than the war which had seemed ended broke out again with redoubled vigour.

[1] A cablegram sent out to the Colonies at the instance of Sir Redvers Buller, before he left home, has been a good deal criticised. In accepting aid, infantry, not cavalry, was asked for. It was explained by Sir Redvers to the Royal Commission that he knew every Colonial could ride, and could be mounted on arrival in South Africa. His wish was merely to save the expense of horse transport.

[2] One can hardly help wishing that there had been on the Tugela a Buller at the head of the Frontier Light Horse. But the Buller was otherwise occupied, and the remains of the F.L.H. were fighting in the ranks of the enemy.

[3] All but one. And it is just possible that had the advice of that one been followed, success might have been attained at slight cost. But the danger was that the Boers might close on Buller's flank and rear and surround him.

[4] Mr. Bennett Burleigh, the well-known correspondent of the *Daily Telegraph*, having ridden over from the main army to visit Sir Redvers' force at Twyfelaar, wrote: 'The camp was splendidly laid out. The men and animals are all looking remarkably fit, particularly when compared with ours.' And a soldier of the Fusilier Brigade which had served under Sir Redvers on the Tugela, and had afterwards been transferred to the main army, writing about the same time, says: 'General Buller is the man for Tommy Atkins! You can always see him up along the fighting line coaxing his men on, besides looking after the proper food and comforts which we are entitled to; but since we left him...last April we have had to make shift with whatever we could get hold of...and no general comes to see if we are properly treated.'

Twelve - Home

ON the 9th November a scene of the wildest enthusiasm greeted his arrival at Southampton, where, among many others, Field-

Marshal Lord Wolseley, the Commander-in-Chief, was waiting to receive him. The Freedom of the Borough was given to Sir Redvers on the following day, and very shortly afterwards he was received with the utmost cordiality by Her Majesty the Queen at Windsor.

After a short interval, Sir Redvers resumed his command at Aldershot, and continued the instruction which had been interrupted by the war. But difficulties were thrown in his way. Pin-pricks abounded. His orders were rescinded, and he was goaded into the incident which ultimately caused the termination of his command. Sir Redvers had been much annoyed by an attack made by a leading newspaper upon a most gallant and enterprising officer who, after many successes, had at last met with misadventure. He felt that the war was dragging on chiefly because officers were sadly lacking in enterprise, and that this lack of enterprise was due to the manner in which newspapers at home held up to public obloquy everyone, however able, who met with reverse. At a public luncheon he took the opportunity of saying a few words on behalf of this officer; but finding reporters unexpectedly present, and fearing it might be said that the real cause of his remarks was bitterness against accusations against himself that he dared not answer, he replied directly to his critics in terms which, in spite of the undeniable provocation that he had received, might better have been left unsaid. Buller afterwards regretted his unpremeditated speech. After all he is not the first man in the history of the world who has spoken unadvisedly with his lips, and the idea that it was air offence against the King's Regulations is incorrect.

Scandalous insinuations had been made against Sir Redvers in the Press. It might have been hoped that the Government would have made it a point of honour to refute them. The Ministers, however, not only associated themselves in these slanders by their silence, but — incredible as it may seem — never asked the General to explain any telegram, or give his own version of any incident. Yet abandoned as he was in Parliament by the men to whom he was entitled to look for protection, Buller's reputation was gallantly upheld by those whose political views differed from his own. A very prominent member of the present Government remarked, 'It is always a pleasure to deal with an inquiry about Sir Redvers Buller; for the deeper one digs, the more sure it is to be to his credit.'

In the House of Commons Sir Redvers was nobly defended by Sir Edward Grey. He exposed the conduct of Ministers towards the General; he tore away every shred of their self -righteousness, and continued:

'Sir Redvers Buller's first simple demand to publish the correct version of a telegram from him to an officer under his command ...after a garbled version had already been made public, is refused; secondly, when leave is granted to publish the telegram, other telegrams for which he has never asked are sent to him with strict instructions to publish them all together textually as they stand; and when he protests that that is not a fair selection, the reply of the War Office is that he can have nothing more, that he can take his choice whether he publishes them or not, and that the correspondence must be broken off ['Hear, hear']; thirdly, all through this matter there has been either a leakage or a publication of everything unfavourable to Sir Redvers Buller, while everything necessary to judge his conduct in a true light and in its proper perspective, and the situation in which he was placed, has been withheld. [Cheers.] ... The War Office...have conducted this matter as if it were their desire and object to substantiate every charge made against him in public, and not to give him any facilities to answer. Nobody questions the Secretary of State's right to remove a general from his command, but I cannot believe that Sir Redvers Buller was removed from that position, after that length of service, simply because the Secretary of State or the Commander-in-Chief did not approve the tone or temper of that speech. That cannot be the real reason, because the speech discussed no question of policy; it reflected neither upon the Government, nor upon any officer in the Army, nor upon any human being whatever; and, although Sir Redvers Buller in that speech defended himself, he withheld everything from the speech that could have in any way touched the conduct of any other man, and it was made in the face of violent provocation. I cannot believe that, after that length of service, a mere indiscretion — mere faults of tone and temper — or want of judgment were the real reasons for the dismissal. The dismissal was peremptory. If it was not for indiscretion, then it must have been for a serious breach of military regulations. What were the breaches of military regulations? That is the point I wish to put to the Secretary of State. If there were breaches, why were they not made known? Why was there no military tribunal to try questions of military law? If it was a dismissal solely on the grounds of the speech — taking the speech by itself — it seems to me that to dismiss such a man from such an office for that speech was harsh conduct beyond parallel. Some of this injury...to Sir Redvers Buller's reputation is beyond remedy. The harsh and peremptory dismissal is beyond remedy and beyond recall. But the worst injury is that which is done to a distinguished reputation. [Cheers.] I am fully aware of the difficulty of overtaking an injustice of this kind: when once set going it speeds swiftly everywhere, gathers force as it goes, lodges itself in every mind, and on every mind enforces the point of view which is prepared to repel any explanation or justification on the part of the man attacked, for fear that the injustice itself will be dislodged. Nothing is more tenacious of life than a prejudice of this kind against a man when once it has gained a start. But that is no reason why it should be submitted to, or why he and his friends should not do the utmost in their power to demand that the case shall not rest where it is. I have been told that it is contrary to the interests of discipline that a case of this kind should be brought before the House. I do not think it is. The abuse of discipline is its worst enemy; and there are times when abuses of that kind must be brought before the House of Commons, because it is the only tribunal before which they can come. Whether the Secretary of State will do what is still possible and set Sir Redvers free to state his case and the facts that support it, I cannot tell. But this I trust —

and it is one justification for raising this debate — that the mere fact of this debate having taken place will render it less likely in the future that any man such as Sir Redvers Buller, or any public servant in his position, should be treated as he has been treated when he appeals for protection to the public department which he has served.' [Cheers.]

No serious attempt was, or indeed could be made, to answer this powerful speech, but no attempt was made to undo the wrong which had been done. The episode is the reverse of creditable upon the Ministers concerned.

Thirteen – Retirement in Downes

Sir Redvers' military career being at an end, like a good citizen he at once retired into private life and spent his few remaining years in the fulfilment of his duties as a country gentleman on his manor at Downes. The idea — more prevalent than it ought to be — that landed property is valuable only as a source of revenue to the owner was abhorrent to the General. "When his country's service no longer required him he considered it his bounden duty to live among his tenantry. It was remarked of him that there was not a blade of grass on his estate that he had not watched, not a cottage that he had not planned, not a labourer that he had not known from a boy.

His home life had always been very dear to him. 'The baby is decent, and an addition to the household,' he had remarked in a letter written some years before; 'I am told that I ought to admire the Rose of Devon [a prize heifer], but I prefer the baby.' And on a General Officer entering the War Office to take up the appointment of Military Secretary, he was greeted with the question: 'I suppose you know who rules here? Sir Redvers Buller.' 'And who rules him?' was the reply. 'I don't know, perhaps his little girl.'

He now had time to indulge his literary tastes, Ruskin and Bacon in prose, Tennyson and George Herbert in verse, being his favourite authors. He had always been a rapid reader, but leisure for deep study had perforce been wanting. Yet Mr. John Fortescue, the historian, observes that whereas Lord Wolseley, Marlborough's biographer, had taught him nothing that he had not already known about the great Commander, Sir Redvers in conversation at once threw a new light upon his character.

Sir Redvers Buller At Downes

A fine equestrian statue was erected at Exeter, an honour unprecedented in England for one still living. On the rare occasions on which he appeared in public he was received with extraordinary enthusiasm. It would be hard to find an instance of public opinion more universal, more spontaneous. His journey to Lancashire was a triumphal procession. Every station on the line was crowded with his admirers.

In February 1903 he was summoned to give evidence before the Royal Commission on the War in South Africa. His masterly parallel between the circumstances of the American War of Independence and those of that in South Africa showed how clearly he had studied and grasped the principles necessary to the conduct of the war. After examination as to the part he had personally displayed, he was questioned on military matters in general; and his replies in regard to the training of men, the Supply Service, Army Hospital administration, &c, deserve the deepest study as the result of matured experience and reflection, and bearing the impress of a master mind. [1] His words made a deep impression on the members of the Commission, who now began to realise the reason for the unbounded attachment of his men to their commander.

In the General Election of 1906 the Unionist party was scattered to the four winds of heaven. The new Government treated Sir Redvers with the respect due to him, and, it is said, would gladly have brought him back from his retirement.

The General took an active part in the work connected with the erection of the statue of his old chief, the Duke of Cambridge, at Whitehall, and at its unveiling was given a place of honour close to the King.

On the 28th February 1907 he inaugurated and presided at the dinner for the Veterans of the 60th, the association of officers and men being one after his own heart.

He was a member of the Goldsmiths' Company, and on the 29th May 1907 began his year of office as Prime Warden. At the Livery dinner held that day Sir Redvers was greeted with loud cheers. In spite of the distance of his home from London he was indefatigable in the duties connected with his office.

In December he was present at an important county meeting in support of the Territorial scheme.

On the 28th February 1908 he again presided at the Veterans' dinner, and, as it turned out, bade farewell to the brother officers and to the regiment which he loved so well. In the previous December it had become evident that his health was precarious. During the spring the disease gained ground, brought on, as some thought, by the contusion which he had received at Colenso. It is hardly necessary to say that he met the approach of death in the calm fortitude with which he had so often faced it in action, and that his last thoughts were for others. In the earliest hours of the 2nd June the end was evidently at hand. 'I am dying,' he quietly remarked; and then, fearing the words might give pain to those dearest to him, added, 'Well, I think it is about time to go to bed now.' A few minutes later his gallant spirit 'returned to God who gave it.'

[1] Sir Redvers' evidence has been published in pamphlet form, Longmans & Co., Paternoster Row, London. Price 6d.

Fourteen – The Last Moments

No one, I think, can review the career of Sir Redvers Buller without realising how well-spent a life his was. From 1868, when he took up his profession in earnest, to 1901, either in the field or at the desk he was almost uninterruptedly at hard work. He had little rest; little holiday. He was a man totally devoid of ambition. His own inclination, after five and thirty years' service, would perhaps have been to lead the life of a country gentleman; but England has never had a son to whom the thorny path of duty was more sacred. His country could not do without him, and he gave up his life to its service. For his work in high office the Army, aye, and the whole nation, owes him a debt of gratitude hardly, if at all, less than it owes Lord Wolseley. In his military career he had this advantage over Lord Wolseley and many other generals, that he began it with thirteen years of purely regimental service; and though he never commanded a battalion, he was at all events Colonel of the Frontier Light Horse for fifteen months in the field, and had a sympathy with regimental officers often lacking in men whose service has been principally passed on the Staff of the Army. His views on a subject were always characterised by breadth and originality. He set himself a high standard; he lived up to it, and expected others to do the same. 'Buller,' remarks one of the ablest of his companions in arms, 'was a first-rate organiser; his mind was always clear; he knew what he wanted; he gave clear orders and saw that they were obeyed.' His brain worked very rapidly. He could pick out the heart of a matter in a moment, and would give his opinion in a brief, epigrammatic expression. His shy manner no doubt sometimes repelled people, but it was not difficult to penetrate the veneer and to be assured of the innate gentleness of his nature. In 1884, in the hospital at Wadi Haifa, an officer of our regiment, so near death that he seemed to be sinking, opened his eyes and saw the stern General leaning over his bed. Then, to his astonishment, two tears fell on the coverlet. The Bishop of Nottingham remarks that, though undemonstrative, he was always sympathetic and ready to help, either by counsel or, if necessary, in a more material way. On one occasion at Kurot on the Nile, the Father, passing by his tent, was cheerily hailed by Sir Redvers asking if he could do anything for him. It so happened that Father Brindle was at the moment greatly disturbed by something which he thereupon mentioned to the General, who at once put aside his own urgent work, listened to the tale, sent for the correspondence, mastered the facts, and then said: 'When I have fairly considered the thing and have decided according to my conscience what should be done, I never trouble myself with the consequences, because I have acted to the best of my ability. Take my advice and do the same.' 'It was not,' adds the Bishop, 'what he said; it was the generous, kindly feeling which made him put aside his own great anxieties and his own incessant work to give me a word of comfort that touched me to the heart.'

Another characteristic was the simplicity of his nature. He would ignore his title and merely give his name as General Buller. A young officer, who had occasion to speak to him at the War Office, apologised for intruding on his time. 'All I am here for is to be of use,' was Buller's kindly answer.

Sir Redvers' was a very fine and rare character, and he was a man endowed with great constructive ability. His chivalrous reverence for women was a conspicuous trait. In reviewing his career, it is not the question whether his dispositions on any particular occasion were or were not the best possible. The moral of his life is his high sense of honour, his devotion to his duty; he was the servant with ten talents, and those talents being devoted to the service of his God and of his country, he left the morale and self-respect of the Army better — far better — than he had found it. It was during his tenure of the office of Adjutant-General that excess of drink almost disappeared from the Army. His moral courage was not less conspicuous than his physical. We see in his character a trace of Lord Dorchester, a trace of Moore, a trace of Lincoln, but it is only with Napoleon that we can make any comparison in regard to that splendid magnetic sympathy which was by far Buller's highest and grandest characteristic. And how deep that sympathy sank into men's hearts, hundreds of instances can be given. Let two suffice.

One day in London he called a cab and asked the fare to Kensal Green. The cabman replied, 'I would drive *you,* Sir Redvers, all round London for nothing.'

In the train — on the day of the funeral — an Artilleryman began talking about the war. He bad, be said, lost two brothers on the Tugela. Up to that point he retained his composure, but when the name of Sir Redvers passed his lips he burst into tears.

It has been thought by some that the General was ultra-sensitive to Press criticism. The idea is incorrect. It was only when he thought his honour at stake that he spoke out. In a private letter, written shortly after the relief of Ladysmith, he remarks apropos of newspapers:

'What I really most like to get is abuse of myself; sometimes it makes me laugh, and sometimes it really helps me, so I am always pleased to get it. Some of the papers are very funny; they first state an impossible thesis, and then proceed to condemn me because my conduct has not been on all fours with that thesis. Others, of course, hit blots. The hardest luck I have, I think, is being constantly abused for the censorship of Natal. So far as I am concerned there is no censorship. X shut up a person the other day, and was going to imprison the editor because he published an article abusing me; but I telegraphed to him, "For Heaven's sake let the chaps go on; there is nothing so refreshing as abuse."'

Towards those who had transposed his dispatches and misrepresented his actions Sir Redvers was too high-minded to bear ill-will. He looked upon such behaviour philosophically and made allowances. In a long conversation with the writer not very long afterwards he talked freely of events. He gave praise where due, pointed out where mistakes had been made and statements had deviated from the truth, but all in a quiet, judicial manner, entirely free from acrimony; and even as soon as the first Sunday after leaving Aldershot, when the soreness could not have begun to pass away, being with a cousin at St. Paul's Cathedral, he whispered to her that he wished to attend the Holy Communion 'just to remove any bitterness.' Yet, in words of Sir Walter Raleigh (another Devonshire hero) when on his trial, he might truly have said, 'All things that make for me are put down to cunning. All things that make against me are thought probable.' But really, for us of his regiment, the opinion of prejudiced politicians is of absolutely no importance. He was good enough for us. *We* are proud of him.

> Lightly they talk of the spirit that's gone,
>   And o'er his cold ashes upbraid him.

The lines are as appropriate to the one hero as to the other. In the case of Sir John Moore the virulence of calumny has given way to admiration of talent too dazzling for his contemporaries. The meed of praise for Sir Redvers has yet to come. In both instances it was the foe that was the first to do justice to the dead. And on hearing that he had passed away, the Boers lost no time in sending to Sir Redvers' family their tribute of respect. Foremost among them was Louis Botha.

It is too soon as yet to assign to the General his place among Englishmen; but acrid criticism is already giving way to respectful comment, and it may be asserted with confidence that whatever the future may have in store for others, it will only enhance his reputation.

> Whatever record leaps to light
> He never shall be shamed.

At the Veterans' dinner this year, Field-Marshal Lord Grenfell and Lieut.-General Sir Edward Hutton paid eloquent tribute to his memory. 'Sir Redvers Buller,' said the latter, 'was, and always will be, a great personality — one who has left the impress of his strong character deep in the minds of all soldiers of his day...The secret of his power lay not in his great intellect, not in his grasp of affairs, not in his powerful physique, not even in his indomitable will power, but in his power of sympathy, in his love for and fellow-feeling with those round and below him, concealed — and therefore intensified — by a certain roughness of manner and abruptness of speech...The well-known instinct of the British soldier invariably saw through and below the surface, and descried the real Buller, the born leader of men. [Applause.] Modest, retiring, and devoid of personal ambition, it was this intense sympathy and love for others which prompted the many acts of gallantry to save the lives of his men in the Kaffir and Zulu wars, and which gained for him the name of the 'Bayard of South Africa.' It was the same feeling which infused his own bold spirit into the hearts of the shaken troops at Tamai in 1884, and again into the battle-worn and overstrung men of the Desert Column in 1885. It was the same feeling which caused the Army of Natal to ignore in the trying days on the Tugela any idea of reverse so long as Buller led them and was satisfied with them. The man who can thus inspire men by sheer force of sympathy and will power is truly and in reality a great man. The makers of our Empire have never sought popular applause. They have been content that history and posterity should rightly appreciate their services. That was doubtless our hero's wish. To us Riflemen, however, let the life and memory of Redvers Buller be a beacon of unsparing devotion to duty, and an example of self-sacrificing thought for and sympathy with others.' [Loud cheers.]

Fifteen – 'Soldier Rest, Thy Warfare O'er'

On the 5th of June, escorted by his old brothers-in-arms, by a battalion of Riflemen and by one of his own county regiment, amid the strains of martial music and the booming of guns, the body of our Colonel-Commandant was carried to the old cathedral church of Crediton.

'Very splendid, very solemn, very stately,' observed a gifted writer in the Western Morning News, 'was the ceremonial with which Redvers Henry Buller, the man of whom Devon and the Army were so proud, was yesterday laid to rest hard by the noble fane in which he had so often avowed his allegiance to a greater than any earthly king...There was a grief that walked lonely amid all that glittering panoply too deep, too sacred to be touched on here. But the remarks overheard in the crowd showed that the thousands of unpretentious folk who thronged the streets and churchyard, nearly all of them clad in the most seemly and sombre attire at their command, [1] were no mere heedless sightseers, but were indeed mourners, sincere if humble, for one who to so many of them had been, not the grim soldier daring in attack, ...but the friendly, kindly landlord to whom his tenants and cottagers were neighbours and friends, with all the semi-feudal and wholly delightful mutual ties of confidence and respect...It was such a farewell as the General himself, with his strong attachment to his country and his home, would have wished to have.'

For all the two miles which separated Downes from the church the road on either side was thronged with people, some of whom had come from long distances to pay their last tribute of respect; and to us, standing in the churchyard as, with subdued tones, we talk of our hero, the surroundings seem to fade away. We are carried back a generation, and in our mind's eye see before us, glorying in the intellect and vigour of his manhood, the Buller of the Red River, the Buller of the Frontier Light Horse, the Buller of Tamai; till the booming of the minute guns firing the last salute startles us from our reverie, and the opening words of solace, 'I am the Resurrection and the Life,' remind us that we shall meet him again only in that better land, far distant, yet rapidly brightening on the horizon of time, where 'sorrow and sighing shall flee away.'

Within the church the chancel was carpeted with wreaths of the most beautiful flowers — the last sad offering that love could give. And never did the magnificent words of St. Paul sound more impressive, breathe more of hope and comfort: 'It is sown in corruption; it is raised in incorruption: it is sown in dishonour; it is raised in glory.'

The indescribable pathos of the hymns, 'Lead, kindly Light,' and 'Peace, perfect peace,' lent a setting to the touching service; and then, as the coffin was borne from the church, pealed forth the splendid strains of 'Ten thousand times ten thousand.'

And so 'we left him alone in his glory,' and took leave of our noble chief and comrade with the words of triumph ringing in our ears:

> Fling open wide the golden gates,
>   And let the *victor* in.

[1] Even the little children had crape pinned on their frocks.

www.ingramcontent.com/pod-product-compliance
Lightning Source LLC
Chambersburg PA
CBHW032026040426
42448CB00006B/738